MW00397940

Skate Your

Personal Best

In the memory of my father, Wayne Foster,
who taught me to always strive to be my personal best.
And to my mother, Margaret Foster,
and my life partner, Rolf Bettencourt, for your unwavering support
and encouragement during this most exciting time in my life.

Sam

In loving memory of my grandmother, Maudie Nessel, and Jim Hulick,
who taught me so much about skating.

Tracy

Skate Your Personal Best

A guide for mastering intermediate and advanced technique, achieving optimal performance skills, and skating excellence

Sandra Foster, Ph.D. and Tracy Prussack

Rudi Publishing

San Francisco

Copyright © 1999 by Sandra Foster and Tracy Prussack
All rights reserved

Rudi Publishing, 12 Geary Street, Suite 508, San Francisco CA 94108

ISBN 0-945213-27-1
First Edition

PRINTED IN THE UNITED STATES OF AMERICA

Vaughan Printing, Nashville TN

Library of Congress Cataloging-in-Publication Data

Foster, Sandra,
        Skate your personal best : a guide for mastering intermediate and advanced technique, achieving
    optimal performance skills, and skating excellence / Sandra Foster and Tracy Prussack. — 1st ed.
        p.   cm.
        Includes bibiographical references and index.
        ISBN 0-945213-27-1
        1. Skating—Training.   2. Skating—Psychological aspects.
    I. Prussack, Tracy   . II. Title.
    GV850.4.F67   1998
    796.91'2—dc21   98-38530
                                                                          CIP

99   00   01   02   03   04   05   06   07   10 9 8 7 6 5 4 3 2 1

Cover Design: Kristin K. Boekhoff

Cover Photo: David Madison

Photography: David Madison

Editor: David Featherstone

Illustration: Terri A. Boekhoff

Production Note: The illustrations are based on the amazing photography of David Madison.

Contents

FOREWORD

I have known Sandra Foster, affectionately known as Sam, since 1974 when she became my teaching assistant at San Jose State University. As a young master's degree student, she demonstrated a deep intellectual curiosity, a commitment to excellence in her work, and an abiding concern that our students come away with the knowledge and tools from our field of psychology.

It was a pleasure to later mentor Dr. Foster in her sport psychology training, and to tell her my stories and give her my counsel from many years of consultation to amateur and elite athletes. She likewise shared with me her innovative work in performance enhancement with athletes and people in the workplace. Recently, we have co-presented programs for elite fencers and have enjoyed working together again.

In developing this book project, *Skate Your Personal Best*, she has integrated the skills and interventions from clinical psychology, mental training, and sport psychology consulting in a marvelously useful reference for skaters, coaches and parents.

My recollections of Tracy Prussack harken back to my days as a consultant to Olympic hopefuls at the USOC Training Center. Tracy is a champion in her own right who brings to this book the wisdom from her years as a competitive skater and her love of coaching. The instructional text presented here is of outstanding quality, taught from the perspective of a skater who has been there.

Dr. Foster and Tracy Prussack combine their expertise in teaching skaters to deliver their personal best, artistically and technically, with an attitude of optimism, self-trust and determination. Skaters who read this manual and use the workbook and tapes will have the instructional and mental training tools for their optimal performance in skating—and valuable skills for the rest of life.

I am pleased and proud to introduce *Skate Your Personal Best*, as a sport psychologist who has mentally coached Olympic figure skaters, and as a friend and supporter of these two talented young women.

Bruce Ogilvie, Ph.D.
Professor Emeritus, San Jose State University and Consultant to the USFSA National Teams for 16 Years
July 1998

Acknowledgments

This book speaks with the voices of our wonderful contributors. We want to express our gratitude to our four judges for their wise and seasoned counsel: Joan Burns, Charlie Cyr, Jon Jackson and Rick Perez. Our adult skater contributors, Steve Goldberg, Molly Johnson and Jay Kobayashi, offered their richly inspiring stories. The skating community is indeed blessed to have parents Gail Erb, Dierdre Fujimoto and Karen Verili to offer their candid and helpful views on parenting skaters. Thank you for all of your time and for your support of our work. A very special thank you goes to Donna Burden, who gave her expertise in the chapter on conditioning. Donna, you are so knowledgable and a real treasure to us! To Elaine Zayak, our sincere gratitude for your inspiring story and all your help. Our gratitude to Scott Prussack for your contributions to the pairs chapter.

To those who helped in the graphic production of the book we owe a great deal. To David Madison, heartfelt thanks for your amazing photographs of our skaters, and to Lynn Madison and Shelby for your help and patience with the hours spent viewing slides. To the skaters who posed, jumped and spun in our photos: Dave Delago, Whitney Gaynor, Darby Gaynor, Rebecca Erb, Linda Park, Benny Wu, Luke Munana, Laura Munana, and Chris Conte. You did a wonderful job and we thank you so much for being a part of our book. To the Winter Lodge of Palo Alto, California, many thanks for donating the ice time for our photo shoot. Thanks to Kristin Boekhoff for her beautiful cover.

Special thanks to our team: Kevin Peeks, for sharing your extraordinary gift for teaching others how to be and to skate their personal best; to John Brancato, for your help on and off the ice; to Louis Vachon, for your quality work and beautiful choreography; to Donna Burden for the terrific understanding and treatment you've given over the years; to Chris Conte, for your creative choreography, music editing skills, and for taking part in the photo shoot; and to Julia DiGiallorenzo for your work with the skaters on and off the ice. You have all contributed valuable insights for our readers.

The editing of David Featherstone has enriched this book immensely. Kevin Peeks has thoughtfully reviewed the technical sections. Dr. John Heil contributed a review of the section on injury management. We thank you for improving our personal best.

Other professionals who have contributed to the research or preparation of the book include: Candy Goodson, and the owners and administrators of Griffin Sports at the Ice Centre of San Jose; the people at the USFSA—Gerry Lace, Maggie Iobst, and Christy Krall. Thank you all for your assistance.

Sam would especially like to thank: the many wonderful skaters I've worked with from the U.S. and New Brunswick, Canada for the opportunity to share with you the personal best mental training skills; the U.S. coaches for the privilege of working with your students Lisa Brody, Casey Litz, Suzy Jackson, Christy Loninger, Kim Micheff, Peter Sasmore, Stewart and Christi Sturgeon, Jim and Kathy Stewart, Monte Tiedemann, and Debbie Varner and especially to Julie Zusman-Lowndes, for getting me started; John Bishop and family for your generosity; Emery Leger, Director of Mariposa Moncton Training Centre; Deanette and Scott Turner, Charlene and Andre Bouchard, Camilla Saunders, Dianna Johnson, and the rest of the coaching staff and parents of Mariposa Moncton. I would especially like to thank Bruce Ogilvie, Ph.D. for the priceless knowledge he shared which prepared me for the fulfilling professional work with athletes and their coaches; and my two partners, Linda Cohn and Rochelle Teising, who have supported and inspired me—thank you for your love and patience. And to Rolf, for being there every step of the way.

And Tracy would especially like to thank: my husband, Richard Fedourich, for your support and much needed help in making this book a reality; my mother, Sonja Slosberg, for always believing in me; my father, Herbert Prussack, whom I have admired my whole life, for all that you have done; Rita Whiteman Prussack for sharing so much love and quality time and giving me a younger sibling to love; my sister, Shelley Zatarain, and my brother, Fred Prussack, your love and support has made such a difference in my life; my brother, Scott Prussack, for agreeing to skate pairs with me when we were little; Linda Leaver for getting me started in pairs skating; Ron Ludington, for coaching my brother and me—you taught us so much about pair skating; Barbara Roles Williams, for teaching me, taking me into your home, and the positive effect you have had on my life. And to Nicky Powers for teaching me about life, love, and performing. And to the skaters who have inspired me. Thank you for the opportunity to do what I love. It is to you I dedicate my personal best.

Introduction

WELCOME TO OUR TEAM!

Welcome to *Skate Your Personal Best*. We have designed this book, our workbook—*The Skater's Companion,* and our audio tapes—*Sound Advice*—to give you the tools you need to excel in the exciting world of figure skating. We also include techniques for enjoying the process of learning to skate well. In this book, we have brought together a group of people to share their skating stories and their expertise with you. Our hope is that you can draw from the wisdom of the experience presented here to help you meet the challenges of this demanding and rewarding sport.

Skate Your Personal Best is written for skaters at the intermediate level and above and their parents, and for adult skaters. However, we warmly invite beginners and their parents to jump in and use this information to help make training more efficient and fun. This book, our workbook, and the tapes all speak to singles skaters and pair teams. We have included a special chapter for parents that presents the thoughts of three contributors who are skating parents, as well as a special chapter for adult skaters with three contributors from very different backgrounds.

Skate Your Personal Best brings together outstanding instructional information about spirals, spins, and jumps along with the latest information drawn from sport psychology. Our advice on technique combined with mental training skills can help you get the most out of your lessons and practice so you can master new elements faster and with less frustration. The sport-psychology information teaches you ways to manage your nerves at competition time and on test days. The mental skills we teach for focusing, relaxing, and adjusting your energy levels are powerful tools that enhance your skating and also enhance your performance in school and at work. Our goal is to provide excellent information that promotes your development as a skater and as a person.

Figure skating presents you with an unparalleled opportunity to become both a finely tuned athlete and someone who moves across the ice with a dancer's grace. The elements executed at the upper levels of competition in singles, pairs, and ice dancing require the kind of strength, balance, and coordination that are the goals of gymnasts and high hurdlers. What makes skating exceptional is that not only must physical feats

1

like jumps be executed, but they must be performed with an artistic presence. It is not surprising that figure skating has evolved into the third most popular spectator sport (after football and baseball) with an audience undoubtedly enthralled by the blend of beauty and physical power.

Someone just starting to explore figure skating usually first tries group lessons, ideally with an instructor who takes pleasure in teaching. Young people and adults who like the feeling of moving around on the ice can then find a coach and begin individual lessons. It doesn't take too long for newcomers to realize the importance of off-ice training for building the foundation of physical strength and coordination that difficult elements require. Skaters who begin to compete soon understand the influence of their mental attitude on performing well in a judged sport. Likewise, skaters learn they will reach the upper levels of this sport only with the assistance of several key people.

Successful skaters have said they pursued their skating careers for their own personal reasons, but they also acknowledge that they haven't reached the heights by themselves. Olympic skaters and National and World Champions all have their teams—a coach, often assistant coaches, choreographers, off-ice instructors who help with conditioning, sometimes a sport psychologist, and of course, supportive family members.

Our team is like that, too. Tracy Prussack is an experienced coach whose students can vouch for her love of skating and her joy in teaching it. Other professionals have recognized her coaching excellence, as was the case in 1997 when the Professional Skaters Association (PSA) nominated her, along with colleague Louis Vachon, for the Future Generation Coach Award. Tracy has also skated her own personal best, even skating at the U.S. National Championships (the 1980 Olympic Trials) with her brother, Scott, in pairs. They had been U.S. National Junior Pair Champions and the first pair team to land side-by-side triple jumps in a U.S. National competition. Although her amateur career was cut short when she sustained a serious injury, Tracy made an incredible comeback, turned pro, and then later performed with such companies as Disney on Ice.

Sandra Foster's part in this team is as a mental training coach for Tracy's skaters. She has worked with figure skaters for several years in California and Canada, and with amateur and Olympic athletes in other sports. While her formal title is Sandra Foster, Ph.D., she has come to be known as "Sam." Sam is certified as a sport psychology consultant by the Association for the Advancement of Applied Sport Psychology (AAASP) and is listed with the U.S. Olympic Committee Sport Psychology Registry. She studied classical ballet for years and also learned some of the very basic moves of skating as a young girl. In recent years, many fine coaches have asked her to assist their skaters with performance enhancement.

Throughout the book, in order for our different team members to present their perspectives on the many topics we cover, many sections of the book are introduced by a person's name. This technique allows you to learn their thoughts directly, in their own words.

Sam: When I first met Tracy, I knew she was someone special. We teamed up to bring her skaters a carefully structured combination of performance-enhancement psychology and outstanding technical training. Tracy also offered her skaters artistic development and off-ice conditioning activities for a complete approach to skating. This complete approach is what we now present to you here. Throughout this book, our goal is to help you reach your skating-excellence goals while developing yourself as a person.

When we first spoke, Tracy was already working with a team of great professionals. Kevin Peeks is a former national and international competitor who skated professionally in numerous productions and tours. He works closely with Tracy, preparing students to have an outstanding competitive edge.

Louis Vachon hails from Quebec City, Canada, skated competitively in Canada, and has extensive training in folk dance. He joined Ice Capades in 1985 and stayed with the production for ten years. When Dorothy Hamill bought the company in 1993, Louis worked closely with her, spending his tenth year as performance director; he was in charge of the show's overall quality and brought out the artistic best from the thirty skater-performers. He is the key choreographer for Tracy's team.

John Brancato, who has his own considerable experience as an amateur competitor and professional skater, works as a coach and choreographer. Here is what Tracy says about how much she values the close working relationships with Kevin, Louis, and John.

Tracy: Kevin, Louis, John, and I each have our own students for whom we serve as head coach. We also collaborate as a team of instructors. We jointly work toward the goal of bringing every one of our students to a place of personal best.

Kevin and I met when we were thirteen years old. As teenagers we skated up through the ranks to the national and international level. We then skated together professionally. In the years we have known one another, we have come to respect each other's talents and abilities as amateur competitive skaters, performers, and coaches. We are truly partners in this teaching process and trust each other explicitly. Kevin understands this sport well from many points of view. It is a joy to work with him on the technical aspects of skating. He really understands what goes into a skater performing his or her personal best.

Kevin Peeks: I was eleven years old when I first started skating, and I knew it was my passion from the moment I stepped on the ice. My mother saw to it that I immediately had private lessons, and she has been one of my greatest supporters throughout my career.

At age thirteen, I was under the instruction of Jim Hulick in both singles and pairs. To this day, Jim has truly been an inspiration to my teaching and my skating.

I also worked with other coaches such as John Nicks, Wanda Guntert, and Ron Kaufman. For years, I competed on a national and international level, and in 1980, represented the U.S. at the Junior World Championships in Megeve, France, with my partner, Kelly Abolt.

I turned pro at eighteen and joined my first show in Puerto Rico with Tracy. After a year and a half, Tracy left to get married, and I moved on to another production in Las Vegas for seven months. After several other shows, I had the good fortune to meet famed choreographer Sara Kawahara, who has worked with such Olympic skaters as Scott Hamilton, Dorothy Hamill, and Oksana Baiul, to name just a few. Through her expression of movement Sara not only taught me how to make my body come alive, but she also showed me the value of becoming mentally tough. I worked with Sara for seven years in many productions, starting first in the ensemble, then graduating to solo and adagio work with my partner, Sheri Marquez.

Now at thirty-six, I feel extremely fortunate to be working alongside and sharing a vision with my best friend of twenty-three years, Tracy Prussack. In the past seven years of working together, we've developed a relationship that consists of compassion, patience, and a bond of trust that could never be swayed.

Through our past skating experiences, we have witnessed the collaboration required for successful team coaching, and we are continuously developing our own unique training atmosphere where the main ingredient is putting the interests of our skaters first. When someone asks me for my thoughts on our team teaching, I say, "Find people you trust, who communicate openly, and who are dedicated to the continuous learning process of our ever changing sport."

Tracy: My colleague John Brancato contributes great support and encouragement to our students. He and I started a summer skating camp together at the San Jose Ice Centre in 1996. We organized the program, brought in others with expertise, and made certain that the program was implemented in a way that benefited all the participants. This was no small task, and we were pleased with the results. John also brings his skills and talent in choreography to the designs of students' programs.

John Brancato: I started skating at age ten, training with such greats as Hans Gerschwiler, Gordy McKellen, Jr., Eloise Becker and Kathy Bird. I competed in singles up to the sectional level and also at a professional level. I left the sport for three years, not liking skating all that much and feeling frustrated that I had started too late. I came back and

Our team—(Front from left) Tracy Prussack, Julia DiGiallorenzo, (back from left) Chris Conte, Louis Vachon, John Brancato, and Kevin Peeks.

turned pro in 1986. Slowly, I got involved in the Ice Theater of New York, a nonprofit company for professional skaters founded by John Curry. From 1986 to 1990, I lived in New York but traveled all over the world performing in many independent shows. These would last one night or one week, sometimes up to a month.

I was a protégé of John Curry's for a year during that time, learning and absorbing the finer points of choreography and skating with one of the sport's true geniuses. At that time, I came to the attention of choreographer Karen Kresge, and joined her for a one-month show in Africa and for her Charles Schultz Christmas show in Santa Rosa, California. Some years later, I did a TV special for Disney, and I also have the distinction of being in an episode of the soap opera *Guiding Light*. I also skated with Dorothy Hamill in her Nutcracker tour before she acquired Ice Capades.

I spent one summer in southern California doing a Dick Foster show at the Knott's Berry Farm. While in Anaheim, I met Kevin and heard about Tracy. She was looking for a partnership and Kevin spoke to me about teaching. I liked what was said and came to San Jose to join them, eventually moving to the Ice Centre when it opened in 1994. Two years later, when our summer program got underway there, it was really satisfying to watch the participants progress so rapidly.

While at the Ice Centre, I worked as the primary choreographer for Rudy Galindo's short program, which he skated for the gold medal at 1996 Nationals and for his bronze medal three months later at the World Championships. I also coached him in 1995.

When people ask me about our team teaching, I tell them how it's great that each of us can focus his or her energies in a certain way so that everything runs smoothly. These days, skating has become so complex that skaters need much more attention in a concentrated form at an earlier age. I feel the only way to provide that kind of training is through a respectful and responsible team.

Teaching skating and doing choreography is a burning passion in my life. It is something I will truly love to do for as long as I can. Now, I dedicate myself to using my passion and my drive to help create healthy skaters as well as healthy people.

Tracy: Louis has brought so much to us all with his lovely, lyrical style of choreography. His knowledge of dance and his creativity have helped our students develop their presentation skills on the ice. He also teaches our students edge technique, which not only supports their technical skills but allows them to demonstrate more flair in intricate dance steps. We really appreciate his work.

As the "home team," the four of us are the main coaching unit, which offers our students so much because we have joined forces. Although each student has one of us designated as head coach, we can back each other up and provide consultation. We strive to give our utmost to help each skater be the best that he or she can be.

Our other team members, Sam, Donna, and Julie, come to the rink to give our students their particular expertise. Early in the season, Chris flies in from across the country to help design programs and to prepare skaters' music professionally.

Chris Conte is a choreographer, a professional skating performer, and a colleague of mine who does outstanding choreography during his trips to California. Donna Burden, a registered athletic trainer and an experienced physical therapist who grew up in a skating family, was also a competitive skater. She is the USFSA Team Physical Therapist and accompanied the U.S. competitors to Nagano. Her contribution is her wealth of knowledge about skating-specific conditioning and injury prevention.

Julie DiGiallorenzo is a freestyle coach and our conditioning instructor. She provides individualized and periodized programs for our students to develop their strength, flexibility, endurance, and aerobic and anaerobic capacity. She started skating at age eight and competed at the regional level. Julie is preparing for certification in nutrition and personal training with the American Council on Exercise. She has trained in body building, and placed fourth in the 24-Hour Nautilus competition when she was only sixteen years old. She has been with our team for two years.

The skaters' parents and other family members form the most important part of our team. All of us value the people who form the core of each skater's support system. Without parents and extended family, skating could not exist as it does. We work in close communication with parents throughout the year, keeping them informed, responding to their questions, and involving them in all the planning and decisions. We salute the families of our skaters!

We now invite you to join our team effort in making skating your personal best a reality.

Part One

How a Personal Best Approach Makes Every Skater a Winner

Chapter One

WHAT SKATING YOUR PERSONAL BEST REALLY MEANS AND HOW IT CAN HELP YOU

Sam: Tracy and I find the philosophy of "personal best" so important that we have based this book upon the concept.

What do we mean by personal best?

We describe this philosophy as pursuing a goal and putting effort toward something because it is important to you. Your desire to pursue this goal comes from within and not from outside yourself, which means that you are not skating just to please someone else, even though you probably do care that your parents support you in your goals, whether in skating, in your schoolwork, or in your hobbies. "Personal best" means that you involve yourself in a goal-directed activity because you enjoy it, not to gain someone else's approval.

Tracy and I work hard at our coaching because we feel a strong desire to do so from the inside. We both love what we do, and our commitment to our work is strong. That makes it easy for us to get up in the morning.

Our experience tells us that young people and adults who skate because they love to skate are likely to enjoy their training. When a skater skates for himself or herself, we see a happier and more dedicated process as he or she learns the technical elements and artistic finesse.

Personal *best skating also means that your main comparison is to yourself. You compare where you are today with what you were doing last week and last year. You look to your own progress to inform you about how well you are doing.*

We are aware that comparisons with other skaters may be useful at certain times when an objective, factual evaluation of similarities and differences makes sense. For example, when your coach is planning what elements need to be in your short program, he or she will consult the USFSA Rule Book to check what is required. If he or she reviewed what elements and artistry had gone into last year's winning program at the regional competition for your level without talking too much about specific skaters, that would be an example of an objective comparison. With this information in mind, your coach could then consider what you could do in your own program for the coming season to be competitive.

For Tracy and me, personal best skating means that skaters care about the *process* of developing the physical skills of skating—a process that takes many years because skating is such a complex sport. Personal best skaters are involved in and enjoy this process of developing skills as much or even more than they care about the outcomes—winning medals, making money, or being offered endorsements. Personal best skating means focusing on performance goals like "I will skate my best during this qualifying competition" rather than being preoccupied with an outcome goal, such as becoming a famous skater.

Sadly, we see skaters who focus on the future and on winning who even become dissatisfied with significant progress in their training. They tend to get nervous at competitions because they are consumed with medaling, an outcome goal over which they have less than total control. They may train to produce the factors that judges will be evaluating, but ultimately, they can't force the judges to give them first place. They also can't control what their competitors do.

When an outcome goal like winning is important to a skater but he or she cannot make that outcome happen, the result is often nervousness about losing. This skater may worry a lot about falling during a competition and then looking foolish. A skater consumed by winning may eventually get tired of feeling so upset at competitions and think about quitting, but before leaving the sport, that skater may be unhappy and frustrated on the ice much of the time.

When a skater has a personal best approach, she thinks about competition in a different way. A personal best skater is excited about getting out there to show what she's been working on all season. A personal best attitude means that the desire to win may be strong, but it isn't the skater's focus while at the competition site. The goal of a personal best competitor is to do the very best possible, as good as her very best practice, while in costume and in front of the judges and spectators. A personal best competitor knows what she can control: her thoughts, her emotions, and her confidence in skating a program that incorporates the factors that judges are looking for—and that are proscribed in the ISU and USFSA rule books.

A personal best skater accepts the reality that excellent skating takes years to develop. Despite this long period of training, the process of becoming skillful can be satisfying if a skater is patient. The process can be enjoyable if a skater savors the moment when an element finally comes together after many months of attempts. If a skater is inspired by the desire to attain a high level of skill, he can take appropriate risks in learning a difficult jump, and risk falling because he knows this is truly part of mastering the jump.

Tracy: In my experience, a personal best skater asks himself every day, "Do I love to skate?" The answer is "yes" when a person is skating to see how much he can learn. When that learning becomes difficult, I remind the skater to stay in touch with the "I love to skate" feeling.

These days, there is a great emphasis in skating on the money that skaters might earn in endorsements, book deals, and pro tours. It can be tempting for less-experienced skaters to get caught up in the obsession for the money that top skaters earn.

What is true is that there are many opportunities now for skaters to perform in ice shows and to be paid respectably for doing it. It's also true that, until more recently, most people who were successful in competitive skating were not that focused on money or on being celebrities. Otherwise, during the ten years or more it took them to get to the top, they would not have persisted long enough to reach their goals.

What I'm saying to you may sound a little ironic. Most U.S. Olympic skaters say they wanted to skate in the Olympics from very early in their skating experience; but they had to love skating so much, and the process of learning had to work well for them, or they never would have hung in there long enough. Thus, it will help you in reaching your skating goals to focus on your love of skating and your desire to do well, and to think less about winning, money, and fame. I realize that it's normal now for skaters to dream about being a star and making lots of money. However, the fantasies of wealth and fame probably won't motivate you enough to get up at 5:00 A.M. six mornings a week. A goal of getting rich by itself may not be enough to keep you going when you have worked on a double Axel for months and are so frustrated you want to quit. Personal best dedication—the willingness to work to become the best you can be—is what I see that keeps a skater involved for the long haul.

A personal best approach to skating means you love skating so much that you don't want to miss a lesson or practice because it is so much fun for you. Of course, there are lulls and down times; these are normal in any sport. Some weeks, your desire for personal best can be higher or lower.

What helps is to remember *that you love skating and that love is really why you began to pursue your goals in the sport. It also helps when you have someone around who cares about you,* who can offer support and encouragement during the down times.

There are many decision points along the way to skating at the elite level. I know from my own experience that when your motivation is way down because you've hit a wall, it helps you to "hang in" if your goal is to become your best—as a skater and as a person. If you are skating only to win, or because someone else wants you to, you probably cannot reach inside and find a strong enough desire to keep going or the courage to try difficult things.

During the long years of training, it takes a personal best attitude to keep coming back after discouraging setbacks. It takes an attitude of "I want to be my best" to keep taking the corrections from your coach, and patiently attempting that jump until you land that Axel. To make it to the top, a skater must become self-directed. How well competitors are doing can't be a source of worry. In the long run, trying to please others by your skating won't keep you pursuing your greatness persistently. Skating to get someone else's approval often results in overtraining before a competition or overtrying during the skating of the program itself. This just doesn't work.

Can you have a personal best attitude *and* be competitive? Absolutely! Skating from a personal best perspective allows you to be much more focused on your own training and your own preparation before a competition. You are more likely to be mentally together than someone whose self-worth is tied to placing first. You are much more likely to skate competitively—meaning performing your very best with great results—when your goal is to skate your very best at that moment, rather than being preoccupied with what will happen in the future—that is, with the results. Remember, you don't have total control over placements. You can get yourself in a mental turmoil trying to figure out how to manipulate the judges, or attempting to psych out your competitors.

Skate your personal best, and you will skate competitively, and skate very well. The results will take care of themselves.

How can you manage friendships and rivalries in the rink? It is OK to want to be the best, especially when you stay focused on being the best you can be, without worrying what others are doing. Your best friend at the rink can be your best friend off the ice. I just encourage you to stay serious about your training while you are on the ice and save the socializing for later.

 You can respect your skating friend and cheer for that person. Your comparisons with any other skater, including your friend, would most wisely be the objective kind I spoke about earlier. For example, you are being objective in your comparison when you ask, "What does the USFSA Rule Book say?" or "What elements and artistry won at my level in the regional and sectional competitions?" rather than wondering what your friend is doing.

In competitive skating, you have the opportunity to learn a great deal about yourself as a person. You can learn how to live with a disappointing outcome and go on to become better for yourself in the future, not to show someone up. You can use skating to understand how to win and be gracious about it, because you recognize how quickly things change in skating. When you win, you can remember and acknowledge the people who contributed to your good result—your parents, coach, and others in your support network.

You can use skating as the way you learn how to support and encourage others with whom you train, even while you know you will be competing against some of these same skaters. A personal best approach lets you be concerned with *your* skating and *your* progress. It also lets you be concerned for another person's well-being, because to you skating means something more than winning or knocking others down.

For me, as a coach, I do what I can to demonstrate teamwork and support of the entire group. I encourage my students to cheer for one another as each develops the highest level of skill possible.

Chapter Two

Personal Best Goal-Setting

Tracy: Reaching personal best excellence in figure skating is like taking a long journey with a great many steps. Skating at the Senior level in national or international competitions could be compared to a long expedition with thousands of steps to prepare and demonstrate what you've learned. Knowing the ultimate destination for your journey helps you decide what roads to take along the way.

In skating, your ultimate destination is what some coaches and sport psychologists call a "dream goal," or the farthest you want to travel in this sport. The stops along the way, such as mastering an element or entering a particular competition, are also goals. These goals help you stick to your path as you move toward your destination.

A goal is an objective you want to achieve, or an aim toward which you will direct your hard work and energy. A goal reflects your desires and ambitions and even your fantasies of yourself in the future. Setting goals from a personal best perspective lets you plan how you can realize your potential and develop your abilities.

To get a realistic picture of what you can achieve in skating, start by talking with your coach, with your parents also there. If your coach hasn't heard what your dream goal is, please share this goal with him or her. Your dream goal expresses what you wish for in skating and imagine for yourself in the future. If you are ten or eleven years old right now, you may be fantasizing about doing things many years from now. If you are older, your dream-goal timeline may be just a few years off.

Ask your coach to give you his or her observations about your potential and an opinion about how far you might go in your skating. Then think about how you would bring together your dream with a realistic assessment of what could you aim for—given the age when you started skating and how old you are now. Other considerations are the amount of time you have each week to train, whether your coach thinks that you have the physical coordination and balance to master the most difficult elements like triple jumps, and how much you personally enjoy the artistic part of skating. For young women thinking about pairs, an important factor is whether your current height and weight may make this kind of skating difficult. Another consideration is your projected growth, or how many more inches tall your doctor predicts that you might grow within the next year or two.

Personal best goal-setting highlights the important role your parents have in planning your future in skating. I encourage you to talk with them about your dream goal and listen to their feelings and opinions about your future in skating before all of you talk with your coach. Your parents have very important financial and time commitments to consider in order for you to pursue skating. They need to hear from your coach about the number of recommended lessons and practice sessions, equipment to buy, ice time needed, and travel that will be required for you to pursue your goals in skating. Then they must decide how these expenses fit with the needs of the whole family.

This talk with your coach ideally occurs at the beginning of the skating season, traditionally soon after U.S. Nationals in mid-January. Sometimes this talk happens later in the year.

If you are skating recreationally, your goal-setting will probably focus on what tests you would like to pass. You may also set a goal for skating in one or more exhibitions in the coming year. You may want to join a precision team. If you belong to one already, set goals that define what you would like to learn individually to add to your own enjoyment and to the skills that you bring to your team.

In our workbook, *The Skater's Companion*, there are certain important questions for you to answer as you decide on your goals. The section in the workbook for personal best goal-setting will give you a place to write all your goals down. In this chapter, I want to talk in more detail about setting your goals for the year. The next several pages contain statements in bold type that are guidelines for writing your goals.

A goal should be something that you have control over, meaning something that you can make happen as a result of your own efforts in your training.
The issue of control is important in skating because it is a judged sport. This means a panel of judges watches you in competition and the individual judges evaluate how you are performing at that point in time. These same judges compare you to other skaters at your level. You also have no control over what conditions you find at the rink where you compete or skate your practice ice, and you have no control over how well the other skaters perform.

You can *exert control over how much you train and how dedicated you are during your training. You do have control over your emotional reactions to things. You can also control how well you focus while at practice and how focused and prepared you are when you perform.*

If you set a goal to win gold medals, you are setting a goal that isn't totally under your control. However, you set a goal that is under your control when you decide to focus your training on mastering the elements that are required in the short program at your level. You also set goals that are under your control if you say you plan to develop your skills that are part of the eleven factors judges look for when they mark for technical merit and presentation in the long program. These are listed in the ISU and USFSA rule books and I am paraphrasing them here.

Judges consider the following when assigning a mark for technical merit:
- Difficulty of the performance
- Variety
- Cleanness and sureness
- Speed

And judges consider the following when marking for presentation:
- Harmonious composition of the program as a whole and its conformity with the music chosen
- Variation of speed
- Utilization of the ice surface
- Easy movement and sureness in time to the music
- Carriage and style
- Originality
- Expression of the character of the music.

For pairs, judges also evaluate how well the partners skate in unison.

Your coach can tell you what each of these factors means at your skating level. Together, you can write goals so you devote lesson and practice time to developing things like your speed, carriage, and style. When your coach is planning and choreographing your program, these factors can also guide the choices being made about program design. When you set goals that help you concentrate on things that the judges look for, you are more likely to receive the judges' favorable evaluation for those factors than a skater who did not train with these factors in mind. Thus, in a sense, you do have more control over the marks than a skater whose program design and training did not incorporate these things.

An example of a goal that is under your control would be: "I will increase my skating speed so that I can skate a lap around my rink in (*blank*) seconds." You might then take a stroking class to help you pick up your skating speed.

A goal should specify an objective that can be observed, so you can see clearly what you mean by your goal statement.

You may really feel that it is important for you to skate as if you feel confident out on the ice. Writing this goal as "I want to skate with more confidence" may sound inspiring, but it doesn't give you the observable information that defines exactly what "more confidence" looks like.

You may recognize those times when you don't feel confident. A lot of skaters, for example, know they are feeling little self-confidence when they doubt they can land a jump or are aware they are worried about falling. Their lack of confidence can also be observed when they skate around and around before attempting a jump.

This example may give you an idea of how you can rewrite your goal in observable terms, so that you can "see " the goal: "I will skate with more self-confidence by attempting each jump the very first time I approach."

A goal should be clearly stated and definite enough so that you will know when you reach it. Set a target date for achieving your goal.

You may want to improve the cleanness and sureness of your technical elements so your technical marks can be higher. A goal of: "I want to improve my technical marks" is desirable, but too vague. Without more definite information, you won't be able to tell when you reach this goal. You could be more specific by rewriting the goal as "I want to land my double Salchow correctly in practice eight out of every ten attempts by the date of the first summer invitational." Now your goal is clear and definite. You have set your standard for attaining this goal—landing correctly, eight out of every ten attempts— and you have set a target date.

A goal should be a realistic objective for you. It should reflect your coach's assessment of your physical capabilities related to the technical side of skating.

If you have not yet been able to land your single jumps correctly, it is unrealistic to set a goal of landing a triple Axel this year, in spite of what your friends are doing. Talk with your coach about what goal makes sense for your jumps. He or she might suggest that you set a goal like this: "I will work in the harness and land my double Salchow within six months. During these six months, I will work to improve my technique on my single jumps so I can begin to work on those doubles as well" (and specify the date you will begin that).

A goal should be framed so you are saying what you want to achieve, rather than what you want to stop or avoid doing.

This way of stating a goal gives your brain a straightforward "do this" kind of message. For example, if your goal is to "stop falling so much on my double Axel," your brain is getting a message mostly about making mistakes and falling. A better way to state your goal is in positive words, such as: "I will land my double Axel consistently, every four out of five attempts by the end of the next six months" (and specify the date). This goal tells your brain what you want to do and plan to do.

A goal should be an objective that you personally want to accomplish and that you are willing to devote the training time required to achieve.

Your coach may be very enthusiastic about your moving up to Novice level and master-ing several new elements so you'll be competitive at regionals in the coming fall. Let's say she is thinking that you should land three triples and two different double jump combinations 90 percent of the time in practice. You, on the other hand, doubt that you have the time or want to train that much. In this case, you don't really want to go after this goal even though your coach thinks it's a great idea. I can only advise you to speak up and say so. Otherwise you will be forced to act like you want something that you really don't. If you don't speak up and say that you don't share your coach's goal, you may come to the rink late or make half-hearted attempts at these combination jumps just to show how wrong this goal is for you. You and your coach should be able to reach a compromise and find a goal that you want to pursue.

Goals should be written down.

Goals are best written down during the discussion with your coach and parents, when you all plan the coming skating season. Written goals give you a reference point; they are like your map for your skating journey during the coming year. Writing out goals lets you see if you are working on something that you have control over, and it allows you to make sure that your goal is observable, that it is something you can measure your progress in, and that you have set a date for reaching it. Writing out your goals lets you evaluate with your coach whether each goal challenges you but doesn't feel like it is too much. Looking at each written goal also lets you decide if the goal is something that *you* want to pursue.

I want to explain the difference between an "outcome goal" and a "performance goal." Outcome goals have to do with outcomes or results, like placements and winning. Skaters who reach great success usually have an outcome goal in mind from the time they begin to realize that they love the sport and have talent. For example, 1988 Olympic gold medalist Brian Boitano writes in his autobiography, *Boitano's Edge*, that he had a lifelong dream of skating at the Winter Olympics. His outcome goal was to try for Olympic gold, and it took him sixteen years to reach this objective.

What keeps someone showing up for practice for such a long time, like sixteen years? An outcome goal like "I will compete at the Olympics in singles" can help a talented skater believe that she or he has something worthwhile to train hard for in order to achieve. An image of yourself standing on the podium at the Olympics can help that dream goal look vivid in your mind's eye and seem like something real to go for.

OK, there is the dream. But what truly keeps a skater coming back to practice each morning for all those years? It is performance goals set at the beginning of every season that keep that skater moving through the process of acquiring the technical and artistic skills needed to compete at the Olympic games.

It is short-term performance goals that show the skater how to improve steadily, day by day, toward his dream. Having a goal for every practice session and every lesson truly keeps a skater focused and progressing.

I know this may sound a little odd, but you would be wise to set aside your dream goal as you skate your practice ice and skate your programs in competition. Focusing on an outcome goal like winning distracts you from what you came there to do—to skate your personal best during your program—which is a true performance goal. Skating your personal best as your goal maximizes your focus on you and what you have control over at the competition site.

Here is another performance goal for competition: "I will skate my long program with excitement, by really getting myself into the music and by holding my arms and hands in the positions my ballet teacher taught me." This performance goal could help you stay focused on you and your skating—which are things you have control over. This performance goal puts your attention on *now*, rather than on the future. If you are concentrating on skating your best, rather than on winning, you can be less distracted by

worrying about what the judges are deciding or comparing yourself to your competitors. Remember, winning is focused on something happening in the future. The future
and winning are not under your total control. We tend to worry the most about things
we have decided we want a lot—in the future—but have little control over. This is a real
setup for being nervous while you are competing.

Let me summarize the benefits of performance goals.

- Performance goals define *how* you want to skate an element, like "I want to pull in
  tight on my double flip."
- Performance goals, when stated as short-term goals for each practice session and
  lesson, help you focus on what you are doing right at that moment. When you
  are focused on working on a particular element or section of your program,
  you will use your lesson time more effectively and are likely to progress more
  quickly.
- Performance goals help you stay on track as you make progress toward your dream
  goal by defining the steps that mean steady and continuous improvement in
  your skating.
- Performance goals for competition can help you control your nervousness by keeping you focused on skating your personal best—*right now*. This will keep your
  mind from being distracted by thoughts about the judges and your competitors. A performance goal "to skate my personal best in the short program" helps
  prevent you from getting upset before going out on the ice because you're worrying much less about things you can't control.

Now, think about how far you want to go in your skating. If you have our *Skater's
Companion*, you can write your goals in the spaces on setting your personal goal or, you
can use a notebook to record your thoughts as you read this manual.

First write down your dream goal. If you have a mental image of yourself enjoying
your dream goal, write about that image.

Now write your goals for the upcoming skating season. If you skate competitively,
you should write down the names of the competitions that you plan to enter. It is also
helpful to write out performance goals and outcome goals for each competition. You
may also have a sport psychology goal for the coming season. Examples might be "I will
learn relaxation techniques to help me manage my nervousness at competition," or "I
will focus more on my own skating when I perform my programs in competition by
learning to tune out external distractions such as what my competitors are doing and
the noise and confusion in the rink."

If you skate recreationally, you may want to list as your goals the tests that you want
to pass this coming year. You may want to state the exhibitions or showcases in which
you want to skate. Or you might list the skating clinics that you want to attend this year.

When deciding about your goals, think about how far you have already progressed.
If you skate recreationally, write out what tests you passed last year. Write something
about how you are progressing in the artistic side of your skating.

If you are a competitive skater, write a brief description of your progress during this
past year. Looking at your progress, write goals for your technical improvement. Then,

write goals for the development of your artistic quality. Get your coach's help in defining goals that include training in the eleven factors that the judges look for in marking for technical merit and artistic expression. You can list the technical goals by category, i.e., moves in the field, spirals, spins, and jumps, or any other elements if you skate pairs or ice dance. Then you can define your artistic goals in terms of categories of things you'd like to improve: carriage, style, arm positions, footwork, head positions, and skating more to the rhythm of the music.

In the next chapter, Sam talks about the mental side of skating well. You may want to add a sport psychology goal to your list after reading this section.

Part Two

Mental and Physical Training Skills for Skating and for Life

Chapter Three

The Thinking That Leads to Skating Excellence

The Power of Optimism for Your Skating

Sam: Sport psychologists are aware that an athlete's mental attitude influences his or her ability to perform well in competition. Mental attitude also plays a role in how well an athlete trains and uses a coach's instructions. As a sport psychologist myself, I have witnessed the connection between a skater's mental attitude and how much nervousness that skater feels during competition. I have also observed the link between mental attitude and how a skater handles frustration during tough times in training.

I am not saying that mental attitude alone can make a skater great. Obviously, a skater must have certain physical capabilities as a foundation, and then do the off-ice training necessary to develop the strength, coordination, flexibility, and aerobic capacity that will maximize the results of on-ice instruction. No amount of wishful thinking, visualization, or relaxation techniques can replace long years of training, and no particular sport psychology intervention can give an inadequately trained skater a magic bullet before skating her short program, even though such a technique might help the skater be less upset about the inevitably disappointing outcome.

Figure skating is a very demanding physical sport. This is clear even to spectators watching Olympic skaters execute triple jumps. What is also clear is that skating is a demanding sport *mentally* as well. When you master specific sport psychology skills (also called mental training skills), you have tools that assist you in developing your physical skills during your training. Mental training skills are crucial in managing the challenges of skating in competition.

One of the main tasks of sport psychology is to teach athletes how to develop a good mental attitude about their sport. Until recently, the methods sport psychologists typically used encouraged athletes to say positive affirmations to themselves and to stop self-talk that was self-critical or discouraging. Today, however, mental training in sports has advanced beyond just the useful techniques of positive thinking and yelling "stop" to yourself when your thoughts are negative.

Martin Seligman, a professor of psychology at the University of Pennsylvania, did the cutting-edge research showing that the way a person explains what happens to him, whether good or bad, is his characteristic way of interpreting what goes on in his life. This "explanatory style," as he called it, is either pessimistic or optimistic. Seligman's work is described in his book, *The Optimistic Child*. I recommend that you read it for detailed information about developing your own optimism.

In the next several pages, I discuss the differences between optimistic and pessimistic explanatory style as Dr. Seligman explained them.[1] I then describe how optimism applies to athletes' success, including figure skaters like you, and suggest statements you can use to begin to make your explanatory style (and therefore, your mental attitude) more optimistic for better results in your skating and in your life.

When bad things happen, the pessimistic person often explains a bad event as having a *personal* cause, like "it's *my* fault." The pessimist takes the negative event personally and blames himself excessively. The pessimist does not consider what other people or circumstances had to do with causing that bad event.

The pessimist feels bad as a consequence of his pessimistic explanatory style. He feels upset about the bad thing that happened and also feels bad about himself. His self-esteem, or his view of himself, is likely to be adversely affected. He may believe things like, "I'm a failure" or "I'm a loser." His low opinion of himself blocks him from thinking about what he can do to correct any mistake he has made; he is unlikely to come up with a better alternative that would give him the outcome he desires in any future attempt.

This low self-esteem makes it harder for the pessimist to look outside himself in order to see what could be changed in his external situation to keep the bad event from happening again. Since he is blaming himself excessively for negative occurrences, he won't think much about how the behavior of other people played a part in the bad event. Consequently, he won't discuss or negotiate with others what mistakes they may have made or what they could change to prevent the bad event from repeating itself in the future.

The pessimist also explains a bad event as something that will last a long time (like forever) and then feels distressed and hopeless about this *permanence* of bad things. For the pessimist, tomorrow never comes; the darkness before the dawn just lasts and lasts, without much hope for a new day.

Along with how long an event lasts and whether a person sees himself personally as the cause, there is a third aspect of explanatory style, that of how much of life is perceived to be affected by the good or bad event. The pessimist looks at one bad event and generalizes his negative view to other parts of his life. For example, if the pessimist is having a hard time at home, he starts to think that things are not going well in school, either, or at his job. Soon, the pessimist is perceiving many aspects of his life as bad. This generalizing is like a domino effect, and the pessimist soon thinks that all of his life is a disaster.

---

[1]The material in this chapter first appeared in an article I wrote for the newsletter *Skater's Edge*, in the Summer 1996 issue.

How much of a person's life is explained as good or bad Seligman terms the *pervasive* dimension. Pessimists see one instance of negativity extending to just about everything else. For example, getting stuck in morning traffic (one negative thing) is upsetting to most people, but for a person whose explanatory style is pessimistic on the pervasive dimension, the traffic inconvenience triggers the negative thinking about other areas of his life. This domino effect of negativity soon leads to the conclusion that he might as well give up on expecting anything going well for the rest of the day.

An optimistic person explains bad events in terms of causes that are only temporary. She sees difficulties as setbacks rather than permanent failures. An optimist views a loss or disappointment as specific to one situation or related to a particular person. Finally, an optimistic person looks at her role as well as the actions of others and the impact of external circumstances in evaluating the cause of a negative outcome.

When good things occur, the optimist sees them as lasting a long time. In contrast, the pessimist explains a good event as fleeting or temporary. He might say, "Yes, I was good today, but tomorrow I won't be."

An optimist explains pleasant outcomes in terms of her pervasive or generalized good qualities or skills. A pessimist limits his explanation of a positive event to that one situation or person. An optimist can take credit for her role in her success while a pessimist attributes his success to chance or luck, or notices the role of others without seeing his own part in a positive outcome.

Let's think about how pessimistic versus optimistic explanatory styles affect a skater.

Two skaters with similar physical potential skating at the same level and training with good coaches, can respond very differently to a disappointment if one has a optimistic explanatory style and the other's is pessimistic. Let's say both skaters have repeatedly attempted a double Axel in a lesson. Both fall several times even though both want very much to land the jump, and their coaches are patiently giving corrections.

The pessimistic skater is mostly feeling angry. Her pessimistic explanatory style is telling her this sort of reason for why she is having such difficulty: "I'll never get my double Axel! It's just too much for me! I should quit skating because I can't skate that well. And my friends are mad at me and my math is way too hard!"

Because she is so upset, the pessimistic skater isn't listening to her coach. In fact, she is ignoring the corrections because she believes they won't help her anyway, since she is a lousy skater. She threatens to quit because her pessimism makes it almost impossible for her to believe she will finally land the jump and continue to learn even more difficult jumps like triples.

For the pessimistic skater training is often unpleasant. She doesn't cope well with the mistakes and falls that are an expected part of skating.

The optimistic skater explains her struggle with the double Axel in a very different way. She can take responsibility for her struggling and falling without blaming herself excessively. She does not label herself as a lousy skater, but recognizes her part when things are not working. She might realize her physical state is part of the explanation: "I'm tired and I'm not focused today. That is probably why it's not working for me. Oh, well, I have our family vacation to look forward to, and it's fun to laugh with my friends here at the rink when I finish this lesson. I can come back to this tomorrow when I feel more rested and can think more clearly."

These optimistic explanations for the disappointing lesson describe conditions (tired; not focused) that won't last forever. They are temporary—limited in time—and she can fix them.

An optimistic skater catches herself if she starts to think in a pervasively negative way. She can turn her thoughts around if she begins to think, "one bad thing = many things are bad." Then she can divert her attention to other things in her life that are going well for her, even if skating, at that moment, is not.

When the optimistic skater is given a correction, she can listen to it and try it out because she sees herself as a good skater whose skating is not going well *right then.* If the skater falls after trying the correction, she and her coach can decide whether she should work on another element she *can* execute easily and end the lesson on a positive note. The optimistic skater doesn't keep hammering away at an element that she isn't landing. She knows it isn't a good idea to practice a mistake; she tells herself that tomorrow is another day and that she can try the jump then.

The optimistic skater keeps her perspective. If her skating isn't going well today, she will be doing better in practice soon enough. An optimistic skater believes that she can fix her mistakes and get a better result without criticizing herself for the temporary difficulty. She can contain, or limit, the negativity that happened in that lesson on that particular morning and go on and enjoy the rest of her day.

Optimists learn their optimism. They are not born with it.

Our own explanatory style, whether pessimistic or optimistic, is learned primarily from our experiences growing up, and we may take on the explanatory style that our parents showed us. We are likely to learn pessimism if our early life experience was unstable or was marked by losses or financial hardship. We probably learned optimism if we experienced a stable family life and our parents were optimists.

Through his research Seligman found a way to teach optimism to people of different ages, from young children to older people, so that pessimists could learn more optimistic explanations for events. Then new optimists could learn to think in more hopeful ways and could explain setbacks more optimistically, and this allowed them to recover and keep going.

There are real benefits if you develop your optimism. You are likely to come back much stronger after a setback in a lesson, or to skate well after a disappointing competition if you are optimistic.

In general, optimists are also less likely to become depressed, and they get fewer communicable illnesses like colds and flu. Seligman's research also found a crucial link between optimism and success in sports. College swimmers from a nationally ranked team took a test Seligman created that showed whether each one's explanatory style was optimistic or pessimistic. Then he talked privately with the coaches and asked them to tell the swimmers that they swam slower in their event than they actually did. After receiving this false feedback from their coaches, the swimmers rested and then were told to swim the event once more.

This time, the swimmers who had tested as pessimists swam more slowly than they did on their first try. The disappointing feedback appeared to defeat them, resulting in less drive and a poorer result. In stark contrast, the optimists had the same or faster times on the second swim. Their optimistic interpretation of the false feedback did not discourage them, it motivated them to come back stronger!

This research suggests that an athlete whose explanatory style is optimistic comes back after a setback. He or she thinks about this result as being caused by a temporary condition, such as a lack of focus, tiredness, not understanding what to do, or physically not feeling well and performing below par that one time.

It is likely that an optimistic athlete keeps his disappointment about a lesson or practice confined to just that part of the day. He looks forward to other activities and thinks that things will go better for the remainder of the day. The optimistic athlete persists in his efforts to succeed at his next opportunity. Likewise, an optimistic skater persists in her training the day after a lesson that didn't go well. She asks her coach what to do to fix the mistake and keeps going.

Do you think that your explanatory style is optimistic or pessimistic? Imagine this scenario and then write down your answers to these questions that follow it.

You are learning your new short program. The footwork is intricate and new to you, and you stumble over your toe picks trying to get it right and fall flat.

(A) What is your explanation to yourself about why you are having trouble with this footwork?

(B) What are you saying to yourself in response to your coach telling you to try it again?

(C) What are you thinking you would like to do with the rest of the time remaining in your lesson?

(D) What are you saying to yourself about how the rest of your day will go?

(E) How are you addressing yourself as you struggle with such a complex skill? Are you calling yourself names, or saying you just can't skate, or are you encouraging yourself?

Look at your answer for (A). See if you are saying to yourself something like, "I'm having a hard time with this footwork because it is tricky and I've never done anything like it before. It is difficult now but I know it won't be so hard next week or the week after that."

If your answer sounds similar to that, you are using an optimistic explanatory style. You are saying to yourself that the footwork is hard for you but only temporarily. In the not too distant future, it will be easier to do.

When the cause of your difficulty is temporary, you can keep going. You can stay with it until you get it. Something new to you in skating is challenging. It is hard to do at first and becomes easier as you work at it. If you say this to yourself as an explanation for stumbling over your feet, it helps you to not give up. Instead, you persist.

Optimistic explanations are crucial at those times when you are really struggling in your lesson or practice. Looking for reasons that are temporary lets you figure out what you can fix.

When you come to the rink three to six days a week, having an off day in skating is to be expected. If you explain that off day in terms of not being your best physically, you are not making excuses if you rest, see the doctor, treat your injury, or do a little stress management. Looking at your physical state may help you tune into a condition that won't last forever, like being sleep deprived, and it may explain why your practice is not going too well today.

You can also look at your emotional state and its effect on your skating. You may notice that you are overloaded with schoolwork or are worried about a relationship with a friend or family member. Noticing these things isn't the same as making excuses for skating poorly in a lesson, if you promise yourself to take care of the problem and come back more focused tomorrow.

When you learn something for the first time, you may need to learn the proper technique *off* the ice before trying it out in your skates. You may find it helpful to watch someone else doing the footwork correctly, either live or on videotape, so you have a model of what to do that you can imitate.

If your answer to question (A) is something like, "I'll never get this footwork. It's too hard for me," your explanatory style is pessimistic. Since the footwork is hard today, you are thinking it will be hard tomorrow, too, instead of optimistically seeing that you can improve tomorrow and each subsequent day. Pessimism takes you to the conclusion that tomorrow looks no better, so you don't feel much hope and have little enthusiasm for trying it the next time.

Because of your pessimistic view, you probably won't want to try the footwork again when the coach tells you to in (B). If your response were more optimistic, you would try the footwork again even before your coach asked you. If you got really frustrated trying it on the ice, as an optimist you might ask the coach for some other way to learn the moves. Or you might suggest to your coach that you take a few minutes to practice something else you already know how to do, and then come back to the footwork.

Look at your answer for (C). If you are thinking that you could continue to have your coach show you how to get the moves right for the rest of the lesson, you are definitely thinking like an optimist. An optimistic skater can stick with it on the first few days of learning something new because he knows he will get it eventually. The optimistic skater isn't worrying about how he looks to others at the rink because he realizes that skating involves lots of tries and "not there yet" attempts in the process of mastering something complicated. An optimist knows the awkward beginning phase of learning a new element is a temporary one.

For (D), if you are thinking that even though the skating isn't going too well, the rest of your day is going to be good, you are thinking like an optimist. An optimist keeps perspective. An optimist keeps her negative experience confined to the one thing that's a struggle. A pessimist who is frustrated during a lesson says to herself that the rest of the day's activities are also not going to turn out well, setting the tone for the entire day to be negative. The pessimist may predict a bad outcome for a quiz later at school, or that she'll probably get into a fight with a friend that afternoon. Optimists, in contrast, perceive a problematic occurrence as specific and do not generalize the negative experience of it to other things they do.

Look carefully at your answer to (E). Here is the personalizing part of a negative event. Are you saying mean things to yourself because the footwork is hard and you can't do it? Are you telling yourself that it's obvious that you can't skate because these moves are tough for you? If you personalized the unpleasant lesson as all your fault or called yourself "clumsy" or "slow," you are explaining your difficulty in pessimistic terms.

If, on the other hand, you are encouraging yourself, you are thinking like an optimist. When you say things like, "You know you can learn things that are hard. You've done it before and you can do it again. Keep going. Stay patient with yourself, it'll come," you are talking the language of persistence that comes from an optimistic view.

Optimistic thinking takes you beyond telling yourself to stop your negative thoughts. Optimistic thinking takes you beyond saying nice things to yourself like, "I'm great!" although positive affirmations definitely have their place in a positive mental attitude. Optimistic thinking skills give you explanations for when things are tough so you can keep yourself hopeful, persistent, and confident.

Now consider this next scenario in which there is a good event. Remember, people have explanatory styles that are pessimistic or optimistic about good events as well as bad events. Write out your answers to the questions that follow.

Imagine that you have skated well at a qualifying competition and win the gold medal.

(A) What is your explanation for why you came away with the gold?
(B) What are your predictions about how you will skate in the next qualifying competition?
(C) What are you thinking about other areas of your life and how successful you are in those?
(D) What words are you using to describe yourself after this win?

A pessimistic skater says he won this time but his winning streak is only temporary. He won't be able to do it again. If your answers to (A) and (B) sound like this, you are thinking in pessimistic terms. Pessimists view good events as only temporary and tell themselves that they won't last; tomorrow won't be good, even if today was.

If you are saying in (A) that your reason for winning is something more permanent, something that lasts, you are using an optimistic explanatory style. For example, if you are saying that you train hard and have mental skills for performing well under pressure, these are optimistic explanations. They are more permanent reasons for your success. An optimistic answer for (B) is that you predict you will skate well at the next competition because your hard work will be carried over to other situations, even if your competitors are also well trained. Saying you will do well the next time also indicates that you probably think your skating well is a condition that will last.

If, in response to (C), you are saying that other areas of your life are also good, you are thinking like an optimist. As you enjoy your medal, you can also reflect on good things happening with your friends and the classes that you like in school. You are generalizing your good; your good is pervasive.

Your answer is more pessimistic if you think that skating is about the only thing going well in your life. For the pessimist, the pleasure in winning the gold is no match for all the things going badly in her world.

In (D), we see the personalization dimension of the explanation of this positive event. If you are saying that you won because your competitors skated poorly or it was just luck, you are thinking like a pessimist. Pessimists have trouble taking credit for a positive outcome, while optimists can say to themselves that they did well because of their own personal efforts. I am not talking here about a skater running around being arrogant about winning, but rather about an optimistic skater who can say to himself that he worked hard for the win and that the judges saw the effects of his training.

Women especially may find it hard to take credit for doing well. This can be true for female skaters who are worried about sounding stuck up if they think they caused their winning. Certainly, it is advisable to be gracious about your gold medal, but, it is also advisable to remind yourself that you worked hard for this win.

If you are dismayed that your answers to these two sets of questions are pessimistic, the examples in the next few paragraphs can help you develop your optimistic thinking skills. Remember, optimism is learned. Now is a good time to improve your level of optimism and apply it to your skating.

If your answers are optimistic, that's terrific. Keep it going. You will also find the following suggestions helpful in maintaining your optimism.

Here are some optimistic thinking strategies for you to use as you prepare for the competition season:

- Say to yourself *often* that what you do in your training makes a difference in how well you perform in competition.
- Set a specific goal for each practice that you skate on your own. Talk with your coach about setting a specific goal for each lesson. These short-term goals are also reminders that what you do in your training has an impact on how you perform in competitions.
- Set a performance goal, like "I will skate my personal best in the competition," and repeat this goal often at the competition site.
- Stay focused on each event as it comes up. Say to yourself, "I will do my personal best in this event" (short program/ long program/interpretive program).
- If you experience a disappointing outcome in a competition, keep your optimistic perspective. Say to yourself, "This is not the end of the world. There is a tomorrow. I will get another opportunity to skate in competition and I will train for that."
- If you receive negative feedback from a judge's critique or from a judge after a competition, stay optimistic. Say to yourself, "I will talk to my coach about this feedback. Together, we will see what needs to be fixed, and I'll make the corrections. I will do something to make those moves or elements better so I can get a more desirable result in the future."
- If you compete when you know you are insufficiently trained, make yourself an optimistic pledge to train more effectively for the next competition or the next season.

If you do not skate competitively, optimistic thinking skills such as those listed below are still helpful for you in enjoying your recreational skating.

- Be clear that the reason you are skating is for yourself and your own enjoyment. When you are having difficulty learning something, remind yourself that you are skating because you really get pleasure from it.
- Keep your perspective about the time required to become skillful in moves in the field and in the elements of skating. Saying to yourself, "I will get this eventually

if I keep at it," can help you stay involved and motivated. Tell yourself that you believe that you can learn to skate well.

- When you experience a disappointment, limit the negativity to that specific thing that is troublesome to you. Remind yourself of the other things that are going well in your life that day besides skating. Say to yourself that this skating difficulty is only temporary. You can come back tomorrow to your next lesson and have another try.

Optimistic Thinking for Skaters

When I'm having a hard time in practice and feel frustrated or discouraged . . .

Tomorrow is another day. I can talk to my coach about working on something else. I can come back to the difficult element tomorrow.

I get another chance/opportunity. Meanwhile, I can remember other successes and count my blessings. Stay with it!

I can figure out what is my part in the difficulty I am experiencing. Then, I can think about what part other people or circumstances play in the difficulty I'm having. I can correct my mistake and come back strong. Keep going!

When things are going well for me in practice and in lessons . . .

My successes in skating will last. Many things in my life are good.

When I do something well, I can take credit for my part and do it again. I can keep my good stuff going!

Adapted from Seligman, The *Optimistic Child*, 1995

As a sport psychologist, I know that optimistic thinking skills are powerful for athletes, including figure skaters like you. Optimism is part of the foundation of a positive mental attitude. Optimistic thinking can help you have a good time as you skate. Optimism helps you turn around the tough times more rapidly, and it helps you recover from losses with more resiliency.

Each skater has a choice in how he or she explains what happens on the ice and off. Optimism is by far the best choice.

DETERMINATION

In addition to an optimistic explanatory style, another key ingredient involved in the thinking that leads to skating excellence is determination. Determination is the quality of being firmly committed and resolute—determined—to reach your goals. Determination is defined as the act of coming to a decision about "fixing" a goal. A determined skater is committed to her skating, and her choices and actions are in line with her skating goals.

I know, as does Tracy, that a skater is serious when she tells us, "I am determined to skate the very best I can." Being determined is stronger than saying, "I want to do this." Being determined means "I will do this."

An example of a role model of a determined skater is Tracy's friend Elaine Zayak, who shared her story for this book.

COMING BACK TWICE—ELAINE'S STORY

Sam: I met Elaine in July 1996. She is blond, spunky, and full of life. She loves socializing with people and getting to know them. Born and raised in New Jersey, she has the street smarts of a city kid. She speaks to you in a straightforward way and looks you right in the eye. She is wise about the world of skating and has experienced being at the top. She's also very clear about the personal sacrifices she made to be there. Elaine's story is unusual and inspiring to me, because her reason for starting to skate is like no other skater's.

Elaine: I was two and a half years old. My father was out cutting the grass and left the lawn mower running. I came out to play, somehow slipped, and fell near the mower. My left foot got caught in the blade and I was badly injured.

I wore a cast for almost a year. I was already learning how to adapt to having a partially severed foot and figuring out how to get around, when the idea came to my parents that skating could help me walk again. So, at age three, my lessons started. I liked skating and got good at it right away.

Having my foot like it was—I was so embarrassed about it. My brother and sister would tease me, "There's the girl with two toes." But you know, I just kept on going. By age nine, I was hooked on skating. My parents had special skates made for my left foot. And I could *jump!*

From age nine, I skated elements nearly perfect. I never missed a jump in competition. By age fifteen, I'd won the U.S. Nationals [in 1981]. I came in second at Worlds that year. I was still young and had done all this in a very short time, and got a lot of attention and publicity.

In 1982, at Nationals, I did all the hard stuff in my short program but missed an easy double jump because I hit a groove in the ice and singled. It freaked me out because I'd never missed a jump before. I went into the long in second place, but then missed three triple jumps and wound up third [overall with the Bronze medal]. Rosalynn Sumners won. As scared as I was after that, I kept going and training. I did win Worlds later that year, but I was so nervous. It was very tough on me.

Elaine Zayak, 1982 World Champion.
© Teri J. Kirsten 1993

The next two years were hard. There was so much pressure to keep going in competitive skating. I was older; my body was different. I was growing up and had to deal with my weight. I thought about quitting. Training was becoming hard. Keeping my weight down was a constant battle.

Sam: But Elaine found the strength to continue training. She placed second at U.S. Nationals in 1983 and third in 1984, qualifying for the Olympics.

Elaine: In the [Sarajevo] Olympics, I came in thirteenth in school figures, which were still compulsory at that time. I had come in fourth in figures at Nationals the year before. I was thinking, "How can you go from fourth to thirteenth?!" I was seventh after skating the short program and felt really nervous. But I didn't want to quit, so I gave it my best shot. I went out and skated a nearly perfect long. Afterwards, I started to cry really hard because I knew no matter how good my long program was, I wouldn't win a medal at the Olympics.

I stopped skating competitively. There were ice shows, but nothing was quite right for me then, being on the road with the shows. And the years just seemed to go by . . .

I remember this so well. I was watching the 1993 Nationals on TV. They were in Phoenix. I was thinking I could do something that would really amaze people. No other American woman had ever come back to eligibility for competition after retiring from amateur skating. Katarina Witt was coming back for East Germany, and pair skater Ekaterina Gordeeva for the Soviet Union.

Seeing the 1993 Nationals, I was saying to myself that it seemed like a very hard time for skaters. There was a lot of bad press about skating that year. There was a lot of talk about the U.S. needing better skaters. I started thinking about making a comeback then.

I had worked with Peter Burroughs because I wanted to train with the best. I looked up to him like a father. I told Peter I wanted to reinstate, qualify for the Detroit Nationals in 1994, and see if I could make it to the Olympics.

Now think about this. Here I was with fifteen pounds to lose. I told Peter, "I'm only fifteen pounds more than when I competed" and he joked, "Which leg?" But that was a *lot* for someone five foot three. I couldn't get my double Axel back at first. I also hadn't done a triple jump in six years. I hadn't done more than one triple in a program in ten years. Where I was training, a lot of people laughed at me for wanting to come back. I was really hurt by that. For a while I thought maybe they were right.

I would not let myself give up, I was so determined to make a comeback. I already knew how to work hard. I already knew how to overcome terrible injury and go on to become a World Champion, when most people said I would never walk again after the accident.

I was determined to come back, even though it had been ten years since I had competed at all. In April 1994, the USFSA gave their decision about who was reinstated. It was me along with Brian Boitano.

Neil Amdur, reporting for the *New York Times*, came around in May 1993 to talk with me. He came again to the rink at the end of May 1994 to do a story about me. Soon after that, my picture was on the cover of the Sunday sports section of the *Times*.

I still had the weight problem. Now it was ten pounds to lose by June 1. At the time, I worked hard on my triples. I did one hour of off-ice daily. I used every minute of my lesson and practice time to get myself ready.

I was twenty-eight years old when I qualified to go to Nationals in 1994. In Detroit, skating my long, I landed a clean double Axel and hit my triple loop. It was a great long program. You know, I got a standing ovation from the crowd, but that didn't matter to me. I got what I came for—my comeback.

Sam: So, what does Elaine's story teach us about determination? When Elaine decided she wanted to make a comeback, she committed herself totally to that goal. Although some people were skeptical that she could do it, Elaine did not give in to their doubts about her. She focused on her own thoughts, letting the voice she listened to be *hers*. Her coach, Peter Burroughs, echoed her own determination and commitment.

Elaine knew exactly why she was returning to skating and her reasons were her own. She clearly specified her goal—to be reinstated in 1994 and compete in Nationals that year. And she showed incredible determination in pursuit of her goal. She was committed to achieving it. Her commitment helped her get up every morning to train. Her commitment also kept her on track with her decisions about food so she could lose the weight she felt she needed to in order to skate more easily.

As the qualifying competition approached, her determination kept her focused on skating her personal best and allowed her to tune out the distraction of people gossiping about her being too old or too many years away from skating to be able to come back.

Elaine imagined her goal. She could picture her outcome goal, seeing herself as a serious contender at Nationals. When she finally reached her heart's desire, she felt wonderful. Her optimism, determination, and commitment got her there.

Chapter Four

LEARNING TO FOCUS, CONCENTRATE, AND MANAGE DISTRACTIONS

Sam: Being able to focus in practice and while competing is probably the best mental training tool a skater can have. You may have heard the words *focus* and *concentration* before but not know exactly what they mean. Here are definitions used by sport psychologists:

Focus—To take notice of one thing in particular by narrowing your attention to just that thing and managing the distractions that interfere. A distraction is something that diverts your attention away from what you want to focus on, like your skating.

Concentration—Sustained focusing for a certain period of time.

I have observed that a person is better able to focus on *what* he is doing if he is clear about *why* he is doing it. For skaters, the why of doing something means that he has answered the question, "What are my reasons for skating?"

You can be more focused if you are skating for personal best reasons, that is, if you are skating for yourself and because you love to skate.

Focusing is also easier if your goals for skating are clearly defined and if you know exactly what you want to achieve in your training. You may want to refer back to chapter two and review your goals for clarity.

By definition, focusing means that you pay attention to one thing and tune out everything else. A skater who is focused is paying attention to his own lesson or practice. Since skaters must share the ice surface with other skaters and coaches, a focused skater must also be aware of his own location with respect to others in order to avoid collisions with them.

Focusing requires that you manage distractions so your attention stays on your skating. I find it useful to distinguish between internal and external distractions. *Internal distractions* are things inside your head like thoughts and images, and the way your body feels. On the other hand, *external distractions* are things outside yourself that can divert your attention away from skating.

In our workbook, *The Skater's Companion,* we give you checklists of the types of internal and external distractions skaters commonly face. These lists can help you pinpoint which ones are relevant for you. We also teach many techniques for how to manage these distractions.

In this chapter, I teach you how to stay focused during your lessons and practice so you can make the best use of your training time. This kind of focusing helps you achieve your goals sooner.

When you socialize with your friends on the ice during training sessions, you are not focused on your skating as much as you could be. Skaters who make it to the national competition level are those who seem more serious out on the ice. They are intently focused on their coach's instructions during every minute of their lesson. When practicing, they stay focused on their goals for that session during the entire time. While some may think such focused and serious skaters are stuck up or full of themselves, this quality of being focused is what helps make a good skater great.

If you skate recreationally, you probably do come to the rink to socialize and to enjoy the camaraderie of others there. Your goals are likely to be passing tests, preparing artistic programs for exhibitions, or learning skills for coaching or judging, but just enjoying yourself may also be a goal. These goals are just fine. They may allow you to be a little easier with yourself about your use of time. Finding public sessions that are more relaxed and social could be a good match for your recreational skating goals.

For skaters who compete at the Novice level and above, the time you have for training is a critical factor. If your coach can schedule your lessons when there are fewer skaters on the ice, the use of your time may be improved because you can focus more easily. You have more space in which to attempt your elements and do program run-throughs. If your practice sessions are also less crowded, you can probably use this time on your own more effectively as well.

If you are a competitive skater, even at the Intermediate or Juvenile level (or below), and you want to be more focused, what can you do?

First, set goals for each week with your coach. Then decide with your coach what you are going to work on during each lesson and each practice session. These specific short-term goals help you zero in on that one thing on which you can focus.

Your ability to focus can be better or worse depending on what you eat. Help your mind be alert for your lesson or practice by eating some protein along with carbohydrates for energy. See chapter six for ideas about what to eat in order to be energetic, mentally alert, and prepared to focus.

Prepare for your skating session before you get there. As you travel to the rink, imagine yourself working on your short-term goal in your lesson or practice. Imagine yourself responding positively to your coach's instructions and corrections. Imagine yourself patiently attempting new elements and making progress in the minutes you spend on the ice. Imagine using every one of those minutes very well, as if your training really mattered to you. Lastly, think about and plan to come off the ice feeling satisfied with your efforts and pleased at the progress you made.

As you lace up your skates, this is an excellent time to talk with your friends there and catch up on things with them. If you are making plans to ride home with them or to do something together over the weekend, this is your best opportunity to discuss these plans.

As you begin your training session, remind yourself of your goal for that particular lesson or check with your coach about it. If it is a practice session, set that session goal in your mind. As you step out onto the ice, use the word *focus* to bring your attention to what you are doing at that moment and for the next thirty to forty-five minutes.

When you train at the same time as your friends, it is tempting to watch what they do. While Tracy and I encourage you to be supportive of your friends' efforts, we recommend that you stay focused on your skating during the session and ask them how they did afterward. At that time you can cheer their successes or offer your "keep going" comments if they tell you they did not do as well as they would have liked.

Successful training leads to competing with less nervousness and more powerful performances, which the judges notice. Your mental goal of staying focused as you train is a personal best strategy that really works.

In our workbook, *The Skater's Companion*, we talk about coping with external distractions like difficulties at home, problems with friends, and feeling overloaded with schoolwork. Here are some additional ideas for managing these kinds of distractions so you can be better focused while on the ice.

Techniques for Managing External Distractions

As you travel to the rink, take a few minutes to clear your mind of the things that are bothering you. If your haven't already made a list of any problems, possible solutions, and people who might help, make a promise to yourself to do this later in the day. For now, acknowledge your problems and remind yourself that you can do little to solve them while you skate, but that you can certainly waste your lesson or practice time letting yourself be distracted by these difficulties.

Use the "mental locker" (Unestahl, 1982) technique for getting control of worries (which are a kind of internal distraction) about external distractions. Imagine some kind of container that has a lid and mentally put your worries inside it. Keep in mind that you can always come back to these worries after your skating session, and take some action to resolve them then. For now, place each worry in the container, close the lid, and tell yourself you can now focus on your skating for the next hour or two.

Some of the skaters I work with have imagined capturing their worries by pretending to scoop them up in a small net and emptying the contents into the container. Their creativity in designing worry boxes has also impressed me. Their ideas include jars with stoppers, file boxes, cardboard storage boxes, and steamer trunks. Create whatever type of container makes sense to you as long as you can access it mentally and can open it to work on the worries inside after you finish skating.

Another strategy you may need to utilize at some point is one that involves negotiating with the parent who usually takes you to the rink. If this parent often brings up problems as you travel to your lesson or practice, ask your parent if he or she could allow you to talk about the difficulties *after* you skate, rather than before. I'm not saying that you speak disrespectfully to your parents, but I am suggesting that you share with them your desire to learn so that you can be more focused on the ice and use your time there more effectively. Then if your parent brings up a problem on the way to the rink, ask politely if you can discuss it when you have finished skating.

What if your worries concern skating? Talk to your parents right away after your lesson. Your parents may wish to call your coach to discuss the concern you are sharing with them. If your worry is about how you are progressing with an element, or if you have a question about your program, then talk to your coach before your lesson. See if you can get your question answered before you go out on the ice.

If you are distracted by a problem at the rink, try to understand what is happening and then decide what course of action you could take. If you are being teased by one or more skaters, your best response is to ignore the teasing. If the teasing becomes physical or verbally threatening, get help from your coach to intervene with that skater or the skater's parents. If your coach isn't there and you feel uncomfortable, get help immediately from the rink personnel. A rink should be a safe place to train, and most of the time this is the case. Do not tolerate someone putting you in a difficult situation. Tell the person to stop and get help from someone with authority.

STAYING FOCUSED WHILE ON THE ICE

Skaters at advanced levels have developed their capacity to focus on their skating through all the ups and downs in their personal lives. Sometimes this is called "mental toughness." I prefer to think of it as being very well versed in the mental training skills that are useful on the ice and in your personal life.

Being able to stay in the present moment is part of being focused. Being "here" where you are, and in the present moment—meaning "right now"—is a mental skill that you can develop to great advantage in your skating. Few skaters develop this skill, either because they don't recognize the benefit or have not been taught how. Tracy and I teach present-moment awareness and focusing because these skills give her skaters an important edge in competition and are tools that her skaters can use at school or when doing something difficult in another activity.

In *The Skater's Companion*, I teach focusing techniques that are well-known in sport psychology. Briefly, saying phrases to yourself such as "now" or "present moment" or "centered" or "clear your mind and be here" remind you to be in the present and help you do just that. These instructions calm your mind and direct your attention to what you wish to be focusing on, like your skating.

Another focusing technique is to take a moment by the boards and imagine the element that you are working on and see and feel yourself executing it correctly. This may be done as a visualization, but your imagining may also be more one of "feeling" the element, or you may think of hearing the instructions in your coach's voice.

For all skaters, the feeling or "kinesthetic" approach to learning is very important. As much as you can, try to include the feeling of the element in your imagining. It is also important to notice which is your preferred way to rehearse things in your mind so that you can use that method consistently.

For example, if you visualize clearly, see yourself entering a spiral using the steps your coach is teaching you. People who visualize may either view things from an observer's perspective or as if they are looking through their own eyes. You may do one or both, and that's fine. Your ability to see yourself executing an element can be enhanced by watching an expert doing that element on videotape. You can also benefit from seeing yourself on tape doing it correctly and then integrating this image into your mind's eye.

Videotape is a powerful teaching tool; you and your coach can watch a video and then discuss how you can execute an element more skillfully. Seeing a video of you skating your artistic movements can be helpful as well.

There are a number of other focusing techniques you can use. If you get distracted while out on the ice, go by the boards for a moment and ask yourself, "What am I working on right now?" This question may sound deceptively simple, but it is a terrific refocusing tool that works for many skaters. You can also use this question at school to get yourself back on track if your mind has wandered while sitting in class.

If you feel discouraged and find yourself distracted, pull yourself back into happier skating by using the optimistic statements found on page 31 of this book. If you get angry about something that another skater is doing, go over to the boards, count to ten, and take some slow breaths. Try not to react, and refrain from yelling at the person. Ask for your coach's assistance if the person is skating hazardously. If you are too angry to get yourself under control, ask your coach's permission to leave the ice for five minutes. Go sit alone and say some calming phrases to yourself. Keep your breathing slow and rhythmic. Talk to yourself about maintaining perspective. Little by little, get yourself back under control.

A performance goal is the ultimate focusing, be-here-in-the-present tool for you. If you set a short-term goal for skating a run-through, you can become wonderfully caught up in skating to your music and getting into the steps and elements. An example would be, "I will skate this run-through as if I were at the regional competition in my costume and I will really move to my music."

Practicing your programs in this focused manner, as if you were skating in competition, is a powerful way to be really prepared when you are actually there. In the four or five months before your first qualifying competition, begin to skate your program as if you were stepping onto the ice to perform for the judges and spectators. This means you don't stop in the middle; you keep skating through to the end. It means you focus on each part of the program as you come to it, without worrying about what's ahead. It also means enthusiastically attempting everything in your program as you do your run-through.

Training your mental skills—like focusing—as hard you train your physical skills takes you to higher levels of skating much faster. When you are focused, you use your time well and look like a skater who means business on the ice, one who can be taken seriously at competitions.

Chapter Five

Conditioning for Skating Excellence and Injury Prevention

Tracy: From my own experience as an amateur and professional skater, it's very clear to me that skaters who are past the beginner stage must participate in off-ice conditioning activities to help them advance in their skills and skate safely. The USFSA has supported the training of skaters to become well-conditioned athletes under the auspices of its Athlete Development activities and National programs. Examples of this support are the seminars presented at the Junior Olympics and the 2002 program offered to Novice competitors at the 1998 Nationals. The current U.S. National programs director is Christy Krall. The USFSA also created a subcommittee of the Sports Medicine Committee to study and make recommendations for conditioning, warm-up procedures, and injury prevention and rehabilitation.

The importance of off-ice conditioning for figure skaters was discussed at the International Congress on Medicine and Science in Figure Skating, a meeting that occurred at the 1997 World Championships in Lausanne, Switzerland. This esteemed group generated a set of recommendations that we wish to paraphrase for you here. The members of this group reported that the conditioning program for a given skater should be devised on an individualized basis. Even when following the recommendations listed below, a skater should work with the coach to locate professionals who could design a program to fit the skater's age, stage of growth, skating level, and current physical condition.

An important conclusion of the Congress was that off-ice training was helpful to skaters in general and should be done to prepare skaters to participate in the sport. It was recommended that off-ice training be incorporated into the training program to develop the skater's balance, flexibility, coordination, strength, and cardiovascular capacity.

It was also suggested that off-ice conditioning activities be designed to help skaters progress in mastering the specific elements relevant to their focus in skating, whether singles, dance or pairs. Another conclusion was that off-ice conditioning should be periodized, which means that off-ice activities are scheduled to correspond with different phases of the skating year. Periodization of training, as it is called, is intended to help the skater be fit and prepared, but not overtrained or tired, by the time of qualifying competitions. Off-ice conditioning was also viewed as important in the prevention of and recovery from injuries to the soft tissues, such as muscles and tendons.

As a coach, I appreciate the efforts of national and international skating organizations to help skaters become better informed in order to make skating an exciting and safe sport. One of the best ways a skater may gain access to this important information on conditioning and injury prevention is by attending one of the USFSA Regional Training Camps. These camps give you the opportunity to learn first-hand what the USFSA has spent considerable time and effort developing.

As a former competitive skater, I personally have benefited from the USFSA development programs, and several of my students have attended the camps at the USOC Training Center in Colorado Springs. Closer to home, I find knowledgeable local people so that all my students can benefit from a comprehensive approach to their skating. One of the most talented and educated people I have ever worked with is Donna Burden. Donna is an experienced physical therapist who works with several other professionals at a sports medicine-oriented practice not far from the San Jose Ice Centre.

Donna is unique in that she comes from a skating family and her parents skated and later became judges. Like many other people who know them, I believe that Ernie and Joyce Burden have made an incredible contribution to skating by providing their time and talents to supporting the Peninsula Skating Club.

Donna began skating at age three and a half, competed as an amateur, and went on to skate professionally with the Ice Follies. She also coached for five years. The USFSA appointed her the Physical Therapist for the U.S. World and Olympic teams. She has served at many National competitions; in February 1998 she traveled with the Olympic team to Nagano.

To add to her knowledge as a physical therapist, Donna also sought out the instruction and experience necessary to become a certified athletic trainer. She is valuable to my students because she knows so much about conditioning and sports medicine, and she is an expert in treating and preventing skating injuries. I asked Donna for her important input for our book so that others could benefit from her wisdom, just as my students have.

I want to make clear that Donna was careful to say that she cannot recommend a specific program for skaters for this book, nor does she do that when she lectures to groups. Her guidelines given here are shared as a starting point for readers; Donna encourages each individual skater to work with his or her coach to find the resource people necessary to design and carry out a program that fits for that skater alone. Such a program would be individualized to the skater's level of ability and age, and would take into account any growth spurts or other relevant ongoing physiological process.

Donna: Skaters need to remember that, first and foremost, they are artistic athletes, and should be in tremendous shape. Skating by itself should not be thought of as a conditioning exercise unless you are doing power stroking, so off-ice activities are a must for intermediate and more advanced skaters to reach their potential. Skaters also have to develop strength, flexibility, and a symmetrical, consistent base [that

Donna Burden (back row, second from left) USFSA Team Physical Therapist, 1997 World Team, Lausanne, Switzerland. Photo courtesy of the USFSA.

is, the midsection—the gluteals, abdominals, and muscles of the back and chest—the trunk] before incorporating specific high-level tasks into their programs. Often, I see skaters whose core strength is generally weak, even though their legs are strong. Individualized off-ice routines used to build strength should start with a prescreening test for the athlete's levels of strength, endurance, balance, and flexibility to uncover weaknesses.

Symmetry is incredibly important, too. There needs to be a muscle balance in the body from side to side, top to bottom, and front to back. An imbalance in the flexibility or strength of the muscles in any of these areas of symmetry can limit a skater from reaching the outer limit of a skill, and may be a factor in injury.

Flexibility means the ability for the soft tissues to lengthen. The most reasonable way for skaters to increase flexibility is to do what are called functional stretches. Functional stretches are not those stretches done in the morning for a skater to loosen up before going out on the ice, although those stretches are very important. Functional stretches are those done at night, or after training when the body is sweaty, to deliberately attain more flexibility in a specific set of muscles in a functional skating position like the splits. These stretches, done with your coach's assistance, help you gain better spiral position, and help make your spread eagles easier. In other words, they improve and adapt your muscle function to your specific sport.

You probably can't do too much stretching, as long as you are doing stretches correctly by holding your position at the end of the soft-tissue length to work the muscles into greater range. A stretch needs to be held, at a minimum, from two to five minutes, with the muscle you are stretching being isolated for maximum benefit. A good stretch is felt, but should not hurt. It is difficult to show the proper positioning in drawings, which is why I encourage you to find a trained professional to help you design your stretching program. He or she can monitor your spine position for correctness. (TRACY'S NOTE: We have only included the drawings of the splits and one other stretch in our workbook. These particular stretches can be conveyed fairly accurately in line drawings.)

I suggest that skaters spend their TV-watching time doing some of their stretches. One suggestion is for you to sit in the splits for a half hour while watching TV. Remember, there is a right leg forward splits, a left leg forward splits, and the middle, or Russian splits. From day one, you could do a thirty minute stretching period by doing all the splits from *your* starting point to help yourself gradually become more flexible.

Off-ice conditioning is a set of activities that help skaters be better prepared to step on to the ice.

The first of these activities is warming up, which skaters must do each time before they skate. Warming up activities must raise the core body temperature high enough to break a sweat. It is crucial in the morning, but it is also important before the afternoon sessions.

I realize that time is a compromise for most skaters. Ideally, thirty to forty-five minutes should be spent in a morning warm-up, with two-thirds of the time spent in exercise and one-third in stretching to loosen up. The minimum time you should be doing warm-up exercises is fifteen minutes.

Let's say you are doing a thirty-minute warm-up. Jumping rope is my favorite thing for warm-up exercise, and ten minutes of it would be good. Jumping rope is better than jumping in place because it's more functional, with more patterning and better foot placement on the balls of the feet. It uses the calf muscles as well as those in the upper body and is a more rhythmic exercise. The remainder of the twenty minutes could be spent using an exercycle or slideboard, climbing stairs, or bench stepping. Be very careful of knee pain if you are still growing, and try non-weight-bearing activities such as the stationary bike if at all possible.

This warm-up exercise should be followed by ten minutes of stretches. Keep in mind that the purpose of stretching in the morning is to lengthen your muscles after lying in bed all night, to bring your attention to your muscles before you skate, and to help prevent injury. Hold these basic warm-up stretches for thirty seconds each at a minimum. Remember, ten minutes will not be enough to develop greater flexibility; to get the extension necessary to do incredible spirals, you will need to do a functional stretch session later.

It is also important for skaters to cool down after the last skating session. This cool-down could include finishing the session by stroking laps with good form and quality. After you leave the ice, I recommend completing the cool-down with some easy jogging in place.

Tracy: Even though Donna and I want to emphasize the importance of obtaining good professional assistance in designing your off-ice conditioning program, we are recommending a book of functional stretches you can do on your own. *The New York City*

Ballet Workout by Peter Martens illustrates the stretches with photographs of dancers from the company. After carefully reviewing each stretch, Donna suggests that you omit just one of them, the Stacked Hamstring and Calf Stretch on page 101, because it will be difficult for most skaters to do that particular one correctly.

The three stretches in the section on conditioning in our workbook, *The Skater's Companion*, are those you can do while watching TV at the end of the day. The first two are the familiar splits. The third one is a stretch for improving the "turned out" position in ballet and skating.

Donna: I get asked a lot about the types of skating injuries I see. The most common among all skaters, particularly singles skaters, are those to parts of the body from the waist down, especially to the low back, knees, and ankles. Ice dancers' injuries also commonly occur in the neck and thoracic area; for pairs, men and women are more prone to injuring their backs and shoulders.

I am committed to helping skaters prevent injury. Overuse injuries are the most common, so being aware of the symmetry of the body, as well as the "symmetry of practice," is important here. Coaches can help by planning practices that encompass every element that a skater is working on. Coaches should also regulate the number of jumps a skater attempts to get away from doing only the one jump that a skater is trying to learn. For example, when practicing a double Axel, be sure to take time to practice other elements.

If a skater tries a jump over and over, he or she gets fatigued, and then starts developing a poor motor pattern, basically practicing a mistake. What also occurs as a result of poor technique is repetitive strain, often in one muscle group. The majority of overuse injuries that I see can be traced back to learning a new element, often at the risk of all else, with underdeveloped strength and/or flexibility.

Injuries may be avoided by warming up properly and, while you're in a growth phase, by doing sufficient off-ice conditioning, especially the functional stretches I've described. Coaches can help their skaters avoid injuries by guiding them in the correct technique and insisting on comprehensive practices done in a consistent manner. Remember, if you don't overuse your body, it won't break down.

Tracy: To summarize Donna's recommendations for the prevention of skating injuries:
- Warm up properly before getting on the ice.
- Learn the correct technique for a challenging element.
- Avoid an overuse injury that can be caused by making too many attempts, without rest, of one particular jump in a practice session or lesson.
- Develop your flexibility and strength in an off-ice program where your training and conditioning needs have been evaluated by a qualified professional.
- As you practice new elements, bring the strengths with you that you have developed off the ice, rather than relying on old patterns.

Donna has prepared a list of questions for skaters and coaches to ask when trying to determine if the discomfort they feel is indicative of injury. She has also prepared a list of suggestions for skaters when they are injured.

SOME WARNING SIGNS OF INJURY

Does the skater wake up at night with the pain?

Has practice been modified in any way to compensate for the pain?

Has the skater been taken off the ice for one or more days?

Has the skater stopped an outside activity (ballet, aerobics) but continued to skate?

Is there redness, swelling, or soreness to the touch in the area?

Has the skater complained of a low-grade soreness for 1 1/2 to 2 weeks?

Has there been an outside injury (ballet, school sports) that is worse with skating?

Has there been a significant increase (greater than 20%) in ice time or jump time prior to this injury?

Has the skater been practicing a repetitive technique for 2 weeks or more? (For example, hours of double Axels.)

Does the pain get better or go away after warm up and return after skating? (tendonitis)

Has there been a growth spurt lately?

WHAT TO DO WHEN YOU ARE INJURED

See your sports medicine doctor immediately.

Consult with your physical therapist.

If you experience pain at the injury site during or after your skating session, stop skating—even if your pain goes away after you warm up.

Stop outside activity such as ballet and aerobics.

Consult with your doctor or physical therapist regarding a slow, educated, progressive return to the ice.

Undertake rehabilitation, if indicated.

Keep your conditioning program going with safe, alternative exercise such as "running" in the deep end of a swimming pool. The water creates whole-body resistance, and the running is a non-weight bearing activity that is safe for growing joints.

If the injury is new, ice it ten to fifteen minutes, every two hours.

Check boot fit.

Check blade mounting.

Donna reminds skaters to "listen to the body and to report soreness" to your coach. She suggests that you ask for your coach's help in making an adjustment in what you are doing or leaving the ice altogether if you feel like you might be injured.

Sam: If you are injured now, please follow the advice of those sports medicine professionals who are caring for you.

In addition, let's discuss what else you can do to help yourself heal effectively and return to the ice in good shape.

- Talk with the professional caring for you (like the physical therapist you are seeing regularly) and your coach about the implications of this injury for your training and for the competitions you have scheduled.
- Spend time with people who are supportive of you as a whole person, and not just as a skater. The findings from many research studies suggest this social support is an important factor in recovering well from athletic injury (Danish, 1986; Duda, Smart & Tappe, 1989; Rotella & Heyman, 1986).
- Plan your return to your normal skating schedule after you have recovered from your injury. This plan may involve several people: your sports medicine doctor, your physical therapist, an athletic trainer, your coach, and your parents. It may also help to imagine yourself coming back to the ice after your rehabilitation and gradually returning to your normal level of training (for an example, see Rotella, 1982).
- Use techniques for managing negative emotions. You may find additional techniques in our workbook, *The Skater's Companion*, helpful in coping with the frustration and upset at being injured and unable to skate as you normally do.

Pain Management Techniques

Sam: Injury can mean that a skater has pain, from mild and self-manageable tenderness, to severe pain that requires therapeutic interventions such as medication. Pain does not always occur following an injury (Melzack & Wall, 1988); but when it does, an athlete may benefit from doing things on his or her own to cope. Researchers have identified different self-administered strategies for coping with pain in general (Fernandez & Turk, 1986; Wack & Turk, 1984). If you are interested in reading their studies, you will find their names and journal information in the reference section of this book.

Researchers Fernandez and Turk described six types of mental techniques that could be used by pain patients. Four of these techniques appear to help reduce a person's experience of pain by relaxing the muscles and decreasing the stress response to the discomfort.

We want to summarize these four particular pain management strategies as possible ways to help yourself when you are recovering from an injury and are off the ice for some time.

In the first technique, you turn your attention away from the pain to something else; for example, you might sit outside and pay attention to the clouds in the sky or the sound of birds singing. You could also watch TV, listen to talk radio, or let yourself get caught up in music that you enjoy.

The second technique draws your attention away from the pain to imagining something pleasant. In the *The Skater's Companion*, there is an exercise where you create a place in which you feel relaxed. You can use this technique for pain management, also. To do this, just let your imagination go and think about a trip somewhere, like going to the beach or on a shopping excursion. In the research, this method was the most effective in helping people cope with their pain.

In the third technique, you direct your thoughts to some activity that is just neutral, like rearranging the furniture in your room or how you might clean out your closet.

The fourth technique involves saying something to yourself, or performing some mental activity, in a rhythmic manner. You could count to yourself in a sing-song voice. You could repeat an inspirational saying or positive statement in a solemn way, as if you were reciting it to an audience. Your mind's attention can be drawn away from pain by both the activity and the way in which you are uttering the words or numbers.

These last two techniques might seem a little silly or boring. They do, however, offer a change of pace from the other techniques; and they grab your attention, even for a short while, when you've tired of imagining enjoyable things or watching TV.

There is also research (Flint, 1991) indicating that observing a role model who has successfully healed from a similar injury may increase your level of self-confidence and self-efficacy (meaning, your prediction that you can do this) that *you* will recover from your injury. For example, let's say you had the opportunity to meet a skater who had recuperated from the injury with which you are struggling. Talking with her about what she did to calm herself, to stay upbeat, and to visualize her comeback may improve your mood and elevate your sense of confidence that you will recover.

Another study (Grove, Stewart, & Gordon, 1990) showed that pessimistic athletes experienced more anger and depression following knee injuries than those athletes who were optimistic. In chapter three, we discussed the many benefits of developing your skill in optimistic thinking. It is possible that learning and applying optimistic thoughts may assist you in injury recovery as well.

COPING WITH THE FEAR OF REINJURY

Sam: When a skater has been injured while on the ice, it is understandable that she would feel afraid of the same injury recurring after coming back. If this fear is not addressed and the skater continues to feel anxious, she may delay returning to the ice. Or she may avoid the element she was attempting when the injury happened. A skater who was injured while jumping might find she hesitates on her takeoffs after returning to the ice, although she may not have done this before the injury.

According to sports-medicine psychology expert John Heil (1993), "the fear of reinjury is always present to some degree" (p. 172). He suggests (p. 173) that an athlete feeling this fear might be helped by a knowledgeable practitioner who does several things that I will paraphrase here (although you will find his entire book a very helpful reference).

The athlete should be assisted in understanding:
- That some fear of reinjury is a common experience among athletes who have been injured.
- That the fear can be managed with self-administered coping techniques.
- That the fear can be a guide in deciding the limits of risk-taking and what is safe in returning to the sport.
- That the fear can be reinterpreted as an energizing mechanism in getting ready for a comeback to the sport.
- How far along the athlete is in the recovery process and what remains to be done.
- That the pain still experienced does not, by itself, signal some hazard to the athlete.

If you have recently been injured, what can you do to manage your fear of reinjury?

If you were injured on the ice and are preparing to come back, it is a good idea to talk openly about any worries you have about the injury repeating itself. It helps if you discuss how the injury happened and what you can do to keep it from occurring again. Your coach and your physical therapist would both be good to talk with about this. If you skate pairs, include your partner in planning your injury-prevention strategies.

When you understand that fear of reinjury happens routinely to injured skaters, you may find some comfort in knowing you are not weird or alone in feeling concerned. The relaxation techniques taught in our workbook, *The Skater's Companion,* will help you to calm yourself and ease the muscular tension out of your body. Helping your body be less tense is an integral part of reducing pain since the impulses for pain and tension travel to the brain through the same neural pathways.

If you find that you are extremely anxious about returning to the ice (beyond the expected level of concern that we have been talking about), ask your coach about the possibility of talking to a sport psychologist. You may need some additional help to work through the distress of the injury before comfortably lacing up your skates.

DEVELOPING CARDIOVASCULAR CAPACITY FOR THE ENDURANCE YOU'LL NEED ON THE ICE

Tracy: Many skating coaches recommend stroking classes for improving aerobic capacity. When you can move around the ice with good speed for several minutes at a time, you are helping yourself prepare for skating your long program with enough breath for a strong finish.

There are other forms of exercise that also help you build your aerobic capacity for maximum output on the ice. These activities include low-impact aerobics classes, step classes, riding a stationary bicycle, or using a stair stepper. I recommend that you check with your athletic trainer or other professional off-ice instructor to make certain that any of these activities would be OK for you before you start. Donna highly discourages skaters from using running as a cardiovascular conditioning activity. She is concerned about the non-sport-specific muscle work, and knee problems that may result.

As Donna tells us, skaters recovering from injury may be directed to run in the pool as part of their rehabilitation program, or to ride a stationary bicycle with little or no resistance in the pedals. Again, please check with the person designing your off-ice program before trying any of these forms of exercise.

NUTRITIONAL GUIDELINES FOR SKATERS

Sam: I am not a registered dietitian or nutritional therapist but have received considerable training in the area of sports nutrition. Therefore, I would like to suggest some guidelines that are routinely published by the U.S. Department of Agriculture and by other organizations concerned with the eating habits of Americans. I would also recommend that you consult with your coach and possibly a nutritionist to see if your diet is supporting your health, and your skating, as well as it should.

Many of you are familiar with the Food Pyramid, a well-publicized way to think about healthy eating. Foods that should be consumed in the greatest quantity, grains and cereals, form the base of the pyramid. The recommended number of servings is six to eleven per day. Vegetables are the next layer up from the pyramid's base, at three to five servings per day. Fruit, at two to four servings daily, is the next layer up the pyramid. Dairy products, in the amount of two to three servings per day, are the next smallest layer. Protein sources like meat and eggs form the layer near the top, at one to two servings per day. At the very top of the pyramid, in the smallest quantity desired, are fats, alcohol, and sugar. These should be consumed rarely, if at all, according to the guidelines.

Skaters may find this pyramid a basis for deciding what to eat. Most skaters do just fine with a diet that would be healthy for a person of similar age, gender and activity level. What can complicate the nutritional picture for some skaters is the desirability of maintaining a lean body mass for both the sake of the appearance on the ice and for greater ease in skating difficult moves such as double and triple jumps.

It can be helpful for skaters to know about the benefits of consuming lower-fat complex carbohydrates, which provide an important source of fuel for athletic activity. To lower the fat content of many of these foods means limiting the use of fats *on them*— like cream cheese, butter or margarine, oily garnishes such as salad dressings, cream sauces, and guacamole. I realize that it may be challenging to keep the fat content low but the taste appeal interesting.

There are some nutritional secrets you can use, such as using red sauce instead of pesto or white sauce on pasta, flavoring a baked potato with less butter and skipping the sour cream, and using jam or jelly on toast or bagels instead of butter or cream cheese.

Here is a list of lower-fat complex carbohydrates (starches) that you might want to try if you are not already eating them: white or brown rice; cereals such as Cheerios, Special K, oatmeal, and Chex; baked or mashed potatoes with less butter for flavoring; pita bread, toast, bagels, and English muffins; spaghetti or linguini with red sauce, couscous; black beans; corn-on-the-cob; plain corn or flour tortillas; and noodles.

Fruits and vegetables are great to have at meals and to snack on, as long as you hold the butter and mayonnaise. Try lemon juice, non-sodium seasonings, or herbs for flavoring on vegetables.

The top of the food pyramid includes the foods you should have infrequently, such as cakes, pies, pastries and donuts, ice cream, brownies, and cookies. While it may not be much of a consolation, there are many lower-fat types of cookies now available, and you may be able to find some substitutes you like such as animal crackers, Fig Newtons, or ginger snaps. Lower-fat substitutes for ice cream are sorbet, nonfat yogurt, and reduced-fat ice cream.

Potato chips, cheese crackers, and cheese popcorn have more fat calories than most skaters realize. Watch out for these. Instead, try baked (rather than fried) tortilla chips, pretzels, air popped popcorn (with little or no butter or oil), and reduced-fat potato chips. French fries are also high in fat because, of course, they are deep fried. For more ideas about healthy eating, you might like Nancy Clark's *Sports Nutrition Guidebook* (1997).

The subject of how much protein an athlete should eat is often raised by sport nutritionists. The book just mentioned can be a resource for you. To determine just how much protein you should be eating, you may wish to talk with your coach about scheduling an appointment with a nutritionist who is a specialist in sport nutrition.

In addition to maintaining muscle mass, protein may also be important to athletes in producing the mental state and feeling of alertness (Pawlak, 1996). "Unlike the calm, almost groggy feeling often experienced after eating carbohydrates, protein may energize the mind. Following a protein meal or snack, the brain is flooded with an amino acid, tyrosine. The brain chemicals constructed from tyrosine (dopamine, norepinephrine) trigger brain cells that enhance mental concentration and alertness" (p. 97).

There is an important message here for skaters. Carbohydrates produce the neurotransmitter (brain chemical) serotonin, which is important for a feeling of calmness, relaxation and well-being. Carbohydrates, as mentioned before, are also important for producing the energy a skater needs to practice and perform.

A skater also benefits from being mentally alert. If you have been skipping breakfast before practice or having only carbohydrates in the morning, you may wish to eat some protein to see if your alertness improves. Lower-fat forms of protein are egg whites or egg substitute, tuna fish packed in water, white-meat chicken or turkey without the skin, nonfat milk, and low-fat or nonfat cottage cheese or yogurt.

Most people already get sufficient protein in the average American diet, so I'm not suggesting adding more protein. However, you might evaluate the timing of when you eat protein and how you might select lower-fat forms of protein. Before trying this suggestion, check first with your coach or, if you are consulting a nutritionist, check with this professional.

SOME CONCERNS ABOUT EATING DISORDERS

Sam: Mental health professionals classify eating disorders as mental disorders (DSM-IV, 1994) because they are not only manifestations of disturbed eating but are characterized by distortion in the person's perception of body weight and body image. Anorexia nervosa is diagnosed when there is a body weight 85% lower than would be expected for the person's height and bone structure, along with an intense fear of becoming obese and a refusal to acknowledge the seriousness of the low body weight. Anorexia nervosa is classified as one of two types: restricting type, meaning weight loss caused by fasting, dieting, or extreme exercise; or binge-eating/purging type, characterized by binges and/or purging brought on by self-induced vomiting or overuse of laxatives or diuretics.

Some individuals may never binge, but purge after eating only a normal or small amount of food. The average age of onset of *anorexia nervosa* is seventeen years, and the incidence is much higher in females than males. It is estimated that perhaps one percent of all females in late adolescence and early adulthood in the United States meet all the criteria for this diagnosis.

Bulimia is characterized by binge eating and then purging or engaging in other measures to prevent weight gain. There are two types of bulimia: the purging type, which involves self-induced vomiting or the misuse of laxatives or diuretics; and the nonpurging type, in which the person fasts or exercises excessively after a binge but does not purge. Bulimics usually have normal weight and experience both shame at their eating and compensatory behaviors that are often done secretly. The prevalence of bulimia is estimated to be between 1 and 3% of all adolescent and young adult females in the United States. Bulimia usually begins in late adolescence or early adulthood and may have been preceded by a period during which the young woman was overweight.

Eating disorders are a serious matter among female athletes, particularly in sports in which a lean body is viewed as desirable, such as gymnastics, dance, and figure skating. Research on eating disorders among female athletes has produced numerous studies that vary widely in the prevalence found. In reviewing the research, Brewer and Petrie (1996) stated, "although prevalence rates have been variable, researchers ... consistently have shown that female athletes engage in disordered eating and weight-control behaviors, such as excessive exercise, rigorous dieting, binge eating, and vomiting" (p. 259).

The effects of eating disorders on an athlete's health can be very serious. In anorexia, these effects are those seen in actual starvation—difficulty tolerating cold temperatures, constipation, loss of menstrual periods (amenorrhea), abdominal pain, and proneness to fractures caused by low calcium intake and absorption. Even more serious are heart problems resulting from the purging, abnormalities which can sometimes trigger fatal cardiac arrest. The repeated vomiting can cause dental problems, including the loss of tooth enamel and cavities.

Some precautions I suggest are maintaining open communication with your coach, parents, and your doctor about your eating habits and your eating concerns. If you are worried about the possibility that you may have an eating disorder, talk with your parents and see your doctor. There are helpful interventions for a skater who has developed one of these eating disorders.

Part Three

MASTERING TECHNIQUES of
SKATING in a Mindful Way

Chapter Six
FUNDAMENTALS of FORM
and Control

Tracy: Before landing a jump or correctly executing a spin, skaters first need to master the fundamentals of form and control. What do I mean by this?

Form consists of posture, the positions of the arms, head, neck, and legs, and the overall impression that the skater's body gives to a judge as well as to a spectator with little knowledge.

Control refers to the skater's command over his body; for example, how well and for how long he can hold a position on the ice. We use the expression "skating under control" to describe a skater who can stop quickly, who can make an accurate turn with a small radius and can do it rapidly, and who can maintain good speed while executing elements with precision and while avoiding collisions with others on the ice. Landing a jump under control refers to making solid contact with the ice without any wobbling or extra motion signaling that the skater is off balance.

Let's take form first. A skater's good form begins with the back. The spine holds up the rest of the body, so it must be properly straight with a slight arch in the small of the back. If a skater arches her back too much, it causes her abdomen to jut forward and rotates the buttocks too far outward. If the skater slouches, her shoulders are rounded, causing the head to be angled forward and the chest to have a caved-in appearance. A strong back is crucial in generating the correct position for the upright spins. With a strong back, the skater can maintain the position of her shoulders over her hips without leaning too far forward or backward.

A strong back is the foundation for a posture that is aesthetically pleasing to the eye and visually suggests an uplifting attitude and more self-confidence. Sam also points out to skaters that the psychological impact of skating with a strong back generates the physical feedback of feeling more self-confident.

You won't find a notation on the judges' sheets for posture, but a strong back and resulting good posture contribute to a skater's base mark. "Carriage" is another term for how a skater holds and directs the parts of his body. Judges recognize the proper postural aspects, both technically and artistically, and reward a skater for them.

The position of your head and neck affect the straightness of your spine. Put in simple terms, keep your chin up and look slightly up (above eye level) as you skate. These two strategies help you keep your head in the proper position, and they allow your neck to feel as if it were long and easily able to support your head without feeling stiff. If your head and chest are leaning forward or downward, your takeoff and rotation on a jump become more difficult, almost like you are working against yourself.

It is not unusual for young girls to hunch over as their chests begin to develop, a result of both the change in their body alignment and because many feel awkward and self-conscious. I encourage young women to skate with their shoulders back and their chest open and lifted. I remind them it is easier to breathe in this position than it is when the chest is collapsed and forward.

Arm positions are different, of course, depending on which element you are executing. When the arm position is not determined by the element, let's say, while you are skating laps, extend your arms straight out from your shoulders.

The shoulders should be the originating place of the extension of your arms, instead of locking the elbows or wrists to hold the arms in position. In fact, you should not allow any tension to be visible in your upper body. The arm extension should look and feel relaxed. I often have beginners skate with quarters on the backs of their hands to gain the proper hand and arm positions. The coins fall off, naturally, when their arms droop below the correct angle or their wrists rotate.

Legs add the final component to good form. Beginners learn that the leg that you skate on is the skating leg, while the leg held off the ice is the free leg. Proper hip position helps a skater hold the free leg straight with the foot turned out while gliding, more parallel to the ice.

Unlike the upper body, where a relaxed and lengthened neck, and softly curved arms and hands are key, the legs are observably taut. The importance of strength training becomes evident when you see a skater with a strong base—hips that can hold legs in the proper position because of strong abdominal, gluteal, and abductor muscles.

These aspects of good form help you achieve what I call a stillness in the body, a feeling of being centered and calming all unnecessary movements.

To check your posture and overall form, look at yourself skating on videotape. Make corrections with your coach's help and tape yourself again. Then look for what you might still need to improve. Ballet classes may help you attain the posture I'm talking about, especially working at the barre so you can see yourself in a mirror. Techniques taught to models who walk the runway also help in training a skater to achieve proper carriage. Models learn runway technique by practicing their walk with a lightweight book on their heads. They must look straight ahead, slightly above eye level, and move without their heads bobbing.

Make a commitment to yourself today to walk tall and proud wherever you go. Sit with a straight spine. Hold your head up as you move about, on and off the ice. Establish your body posture as one that is consistently erect and self-confident. This will help you look and feel great in the rink and enhance your sense of confidence out in the world.

When you acquire the fundamentals of good form, you are more likely to skate under control. Beginners learn about inside and outside edges, meaning skating on the inside or outside of the blade. What helps a beginner feel in control more quickly are deep bends of the knee done in a relaxed way. I use the idea of skating down into the knees so you can skate down into the ice and feel connected to it, giving you a good feeling of control.

Beginning skaters also learn drills that increase edge control as a prerequisite to other maneuvers. I teach them to skate sustained edges, meaning long, extended glides on the ice. These are done at first while moving slowly across the rink. Gradually, the skater increases his speed.

Because of the way that blades are constructed, a skater can rock forward and backward on the curved part of the blade. The term *rocker* applies to this curvature in a figure skate's blade. Rocker also refers to a turn in which the skater changes from forward to backward or from backward to forward while staying on the same edge, and turning into the curve she has just skated.

Where on the blade a skater puts her weight has a definite impact on the kind of movement she will make. For example, in spins, the weight should rest directly on the ball of the foot rather than on the forward or backward part of the blade. If you notice the etching (or tracings) of the blade on the ice after a spin, the circles are quite small if the skater executed the spin correctly, that is, with the weight on the ball of the foot. If the skater is leaning on the back of the blade, you'll notice etchings of circles with too large a radius. The resulting spin is also too slow.

"Soft knees" is an expression I use to describe how a skater can achieve sufficient bend to move easily and under control. Stretches that improve the flexibility of the knees help make this deep knee bend possible, as does work at the barre (lots of pliés!) in a ballet class. When the knee joint is stiff, it inhibits the bend that lets a skater make good contact with the ice. A physical therapist may need to recommend specific exercises to increase the range of motion if a beginner's knees are stiff.

To further enhance the sense of control, I teach the techniques of how to stop fast, and I reinforce these basics in every beginner's lesson. Stopping, whether with a snow plow or a fancy tango stop, always requires the skater to apply pressure down into the blades. Some types of stops involve turning sharply or slowing the momentum by changing the direction of the blades. A skater who cannot stop quickly while skating forward or backward is skating out of control and is a hazard on the ice. I caution my newer students that stops are trickier when their blades have just been sharpened or when they are excessively dull and need to be sharpened.

The basics of stopping and the simpler techniques for turning are best taught in sessions that separate beginners from intermediate skaters. Beginners need to practice these fundamentals of control for weeks, even months, in an environment where they feel safe to develop their maneuverability at their own pace.

Another crucial factor in skating under control is balance. A skater who feels a strong and solid center of gravity can maintain vertical as well as other positions more easily. Balance can be affected by many things, including the proper functioning of the inner ear where the body's important balancing mechanism, like a sort of internal gyroscope, is located. Balance is also affected by the skater's awareness of where his body is located in space both with his eyes open and closed. Beginning skaters who have poorly developed balance find it very difficult to feel comfortable even when gliding across the ice, much less when trying jumps.

When I see a skater is off balance, I look first for lack of proper knee bend. Then I look for lack of the proper position of head, neck, or arms. Any of these can be the result of limited flexibility. If the skater has good knee bend and proper position, I then suggest that his mental focus is not on his skating. He may be distracted by something upsetting that unsettles his balance. He may be feeling fearful and literally have his "back up," which makes the shoulders rise up toward the earlobes. The tension in the upper body resulting from fear can hamper a skater's balance and affect timing and awareness of position in space.

Another idea I teach is that of maintaining dual focus on the ice. A skater must be aware of her own speed and position on the ice; at the same time, she must have peripheral focus on where others on the ice are located and have a sense of where they are headed. A skater can enhance her sense of control by having the mental *intention* to be in control and imagine that her movements can be effortless. I teach this combination of mental and physical control in lessons, and I encourage skaters to practice with mental intentionality. This technique also translates well into skating under control and with self-confidence during competitions.

Special activities in off-ice conditioning can help improve a skater's sense of position in space and improve balance. Preliminary conditioning may be necessary before a skater can learn elements that require excellent balance, such as spins and jumps.

Another analogy I share with skaters who need to develop greater confidence as they skate is to suggest that skating can be thought of as a video game. The skater is firing himself at a target, a particular location on the ice where he is going to execute an element. I send him on his mission, to skate like he means it and to land the jump or complete a spin accurately. I ask the skater to move quickly and under control, making his presence known so everyone else on the ice feels how deliberate he is. They are likely to get out of the way instinctively, because no one wants to be hit by a skater who looks confident and speeds forward with great trust in himself. Skating slowly into a jump is not likely to be taken seriously, I explain, and other skaters may not feel it necessary to move out of the way.

I know it is my responsibility to educate my students about right-of-way and use of the ice. It is also my responsibility as a coach to speak to skaters practicing without their coaches or being coached by their parents if these skaters are doing something that is hazardous. For instance, if I observe a skater fall and lay on the ice, I speak to him or her about being a hazard with this behavior. I tell that skater to get up quickly and move out of the way before a collision occurs.

I teach my older or more experienced skaters that they have a responsibility not to skate too close to younger or less-experienced skaters, since they may startle them and contribute to a fall. I remind them to glance over their shoulders before throwing their free leg up and to practice difficult elements when the sessions are lighter, or near the beginning or end of more crowded sessions.

I teach my new skaters to be energy efficient in their movements on the ice. One analogy I use after skaters have developed some control is that of skating across velvet.

They are to imagine they are skating lightly over it with good contact but without ripping or scratching the fabric. I remind them that the judges are listening for the sounds that blades make as well as evaluating visually what a skater does. Smooth edges sound clean and clear. Scraping or picking noises suggest that a skater lacks control and alerts the judges to look for this possibility.

Chapter Seven
Spirals and Spins with Pizzazz

Tracy: In this chapter on spins and spirals, I share the methods and techniques I use when coaching my aspiring skaters. The skaters you see pictured in this chapter and the chapters on jumps and pair skating are either current or former students of mine. My colleague, professional skater Chris Conte, also participated in the technique photographs. In the following list of the amateur skaters depicted, I include their age at the time of these photographs were taken and a brief summary of their accomplishments.

- David Delago, 23; Senior Pair, Junior Pairs national competitor, Novice singles and pairs national competitor.
- Rebecca Erb, 14; Junior Lady, Novice lady national competitor, and Junior Pairs national and international competitor.
- Darby Gaynor, 13; Novice Lady international competitor, Junior Pairs national competitor.
- Whitney Gaynor, 16; Junior Lady, Senior Pair, Junior Pairs national competitor.
- Laura Munana, 16; Novice Pairs and Novice Dance national competitor, Junior Dance.
- Luke Munana, 19; Novice Pairs and Novice Dance national competitor, Junior Dance.
- Linda Park, 8, Preliminary Lady.
- Benny Wu, 15, Novice Man national competitor.

These skaters, although highly accomplished, see themselves as works in progress and their training as ongoing. They continue to strive for better execution and more consistency in their technique, just as I work to become more technically aware as a coach. In my instructions here, I give you the steps I use with my students to help them develop their personal best. These instructions, when properly executed, represent the ideal that my skaters and I are striving for.

The technical instructions in this and the following chapter are geared for skaters at the Intermediate level and higher. Therefore, I am making the assumption that you, the skater, have already established the direction in which you spin and jump. If you are a beginner your coach can help you determine in which direction you will most successfully spin and jump.

SPIRALS

When a spiral is performed properly, it is one of the more beautiful elements to watch. To make *your* spirals graceful, I feel you must learn the correct positions, reach as full an extension as possible, demonstrate good edge quality, and achieve an awareness of your body alignment.

Your spirals, like your spins and jumps, continue to improve if your training and commitment are consistent and if you work on your passive and active flexibility daily in both on- and off-ice activities.

All the possible variations for spirals are: right forward outside, left forward outside, right forward inside, left forward inside, right back outside, left back outside, right back inside, and left back inside.

When I work on spirals with a student, I like to begin by taking her to the plexiglas above the boards and asking her to pay close attention to positioning.

As the skater observes her visual image at the railing, I ask her to stand in a T position, with both hands resting on the railing for support and balance. There should be enough space between the skater and the railing for her to move freely into the spiral position. I then ask her to stand tall with the head lifted and in a neutral position, notice her reflection, and answer these questions:

- Are your shoulders down, chest lifted, and back straight?
- Are your hips and shoulders in alignment?
- Are your feet positioned in the correct angle—a T position?
- Are your feet aligned under the hips and shoulders?

Try this positioning for yourself with spirals and answer these questions as you do. If you achieved this position and were ready to proceed into the spiral position, I would say, "Continue watching your reflection while lifting your leg straight back with your free foot turned out and the toe pointed. You should feel the muscles stretching and lengthening as you raise and extend your free leg directly behind your hip while standing upright over your skating foot. Now maintain the tall upper-body position, bringing your head forward and keeping your chin lifted while lowering your chest toward the ice." Your free leg should reach its full extension with your arms stretched and lengthened, complementing the line of the spiral. You should achieve this position with a controlled fluid motion that is pleasing to watch from start to finish.

When you have mastered this technique at the railing on both your right and left sides, do this same movement across the width of the rink. Starting in a T position, skate across the painted line and continue to look straight ahead into the Plexiglas so that you can check your position as you glide across the ice. You should feel balanced on the flat of the back of your blade during this exercise, with your weight centered as you glide forward. This exercise can be practiced skating forward and backward. Your weight should be distributed over the flat of your blade toward the center to the front as you're gliding backward.

Spirals

Right Forward Outside Spiral. (Whitney Gaynor)
© *David Madison 1998*

Left Forward Outside Spiral. (Linda Park)
© *David Madison 1998*

Right Forward Inside Spiral. (Benny Wu)
© *David Madison 1998*

Left Forward Inside Spiral. (Linda Park)
© *David Madison 1998*

Right Back Outside Spiral. (Linda Park)
© David Madison 1998

Right Back Inside Spiral. (Whitney Gaynor)
© David Madison 1998

Left Back Outside Spiral. (Benny Wu)
© David Madison 1998

Left Back Inside Spiral. (Whitney Gaynor)
© David Madison 1998

This exercise is challenging. The next step is to try it on the red circle while maintaining proper positioning and control. You then need to learn to glide in the spiral position on all four edges, both forward and backward, while staying in alignment over the curve.

Spiral sequences are required in the short and long programs in the Novice, Junior, and Senior Ladies events as well as in the Pair short and long programs. You can add a great deal to your programs by mastering a broad range of spirals with sequences that are interesting and evenly developed.

I encourage you to start skating large, open patterns, both forward and backward and clockwise and counterclockwise, utilizing the entire ice surface. I coach my skaters to push the spirals out and around on an increasingly larger arc while maintaining the spiral position, and to do this until the speed decreases to a standstill or until the skater can no longer hold the proper alignment. These exercises assist my students in developing the flow, positioning, and the strength necessary to execute all eight spirals. Try this for yourself to become more skillful.

SPINS

The instructions given here for spins are general and apply to skaters who spin in either direction. For one spin—the flying camel—right and left directions are designated.

The following pages feature several spins. The spins are described as I teach them. There is also a photograph taken during the spin and several illustrations which show you the important steps in achieving the spin. In the descriptions, letters that appear in parentheses refer to a specific illustration of the element.

SCRATCH SPIN

While there are many ways to enter into a scratch spin, I use a back crossover to begin the entry edge into the scratch spin. This is a standard setup for all spins. I like to see a skater really stretch and bring the back inside edge around on the curve, rotating the shoulders and stretching the arms out parallel to the ice.

(A) The free leg is extended and crossed under the supporting leg, stretching to the outside of the back inside preparation edge. You should be using a deep knee bend and pressing down onto the ball of your foot. From this position, bring your free leg into the curve and maintain a good rotational stretch with your upper body lifted.

(B) Push onto the forward outside edge, staying down in your knees and completely extending your pushing foot back behind the entry edge into the spin, creating a wide but centered push into the curve. Press down into the ice onto the ball of your foot. Pull your leading arm back and follow it, and then bring your free leg and arm around together into the neutral and upright position.

The forward outside edge will be a tight curve that comes around into the three turn. Pressing down into the ball of the foot with good knee bend makes for a controlled entry. When your edge hits the toe, you rise up in your knee while pressing down into the ball of the foot to center the spin on top of the three turn.

(C) Assume the upright position. Your arms and free leg are extended out, your hips are tucked under and in line with your shoulders. Your back is straight, chest lifted, and head held erect. (D) From this upright position, bring your free leg into the bent leg position holding the arms out.

(E) Your free foot comes in above your spinning knee. Bring your arms to the center of your chest, and then clasp your hands. (G) Your free leg pushes down from the heel as your arms push up over your head (or down) simultaneously while you continue to press into the ball of the spinning foot. To exit the spin, uncross your feet, open your arms, bend your knees, and push out away from the spin on the back outside edge. Stretch and hold this exit position.

Scratch Spin—Linda Park
©David Madison 1998

BACK SCRATCH SPIN

Bend your knees and push onto the forward inside edge of the leg on which you will be spinning. Extend your free leg from the push. Staying down in your knee bend, follow the inside edge around on the curve into the three turn. As the inside edge hits the toe at the top of the three turn, lift your free leg in front with your arms extended out.

(A) Press down into the ball of your foot to center the spin. Keep your hips under and in line with your shoulders. Center the ball of your foot directly under the skating hip. (B) Bring your free leg in, bending it below your skating knee, and then bring your arms into the center of the chest. Clasp your hands. For variations you can either push your arms down or over your head. (C) Push your free leg down to the crossed ankle position. (D) Squeeze this position tightly to increase your spinning speed. Continue to stretch and hold your position still. To exit, uncross your feet, extend your arms and bend your skating knee. Stretch your free leg back over the outside edge.

Back Scratch Spin—Darby Gaynor
©David Madison 1998

A.

B.

C.

D.

E.

Sit Spin

Using the same preparation I described for the entry of the scratch spin, (A) push from the back inside edge onto the forward outside edge. (B) Stretch your pushing leg (or free leg) back, staying down low in your knee and pressing down into the outside edge into the ball of your foot.

Pull your leading arm back and follow it. Bring the free side around, with your chest forward, into the sit position. (C) Your free leg should swing wide in a circular motion, and the sit position should be achieved in just two counts. The first count is the push and then following the outside edge. The second count occurs as the edge hits the toe and the sit position is assumed.

(D) Your upper body must come forward while your free leg and arms come around into the sit position. Your arm position is optional. However, your head and the chest stay lifted, with your shoulders down, as your free leg stretches with your toe turned out and pointed. (This is such a pleasing position!) Hold your body still and tight to maintain speed and press down on the ball of your foot.

To exit, come upright, open your arms, bend your knees, and push back away from the spin. Hold your exit position on the back outside edge and stretch.

Sit Spin—Rebecca Erb
©David Madison 1998

CAMEL SPIN

From a push onto the forward outside edge, extend your free leg back, bringing your upper body forward with your chest out over the skating knee. Press down into the ice with the forward outside edge, pulling your leading arm back. Follow your arm, bringing the forward outside edge around into the three turn.

(D) Keep your free leg stretched back over the entry edge and lift your leg into the camel position as your edge comes around to your toe. (E) Press on the ball of your foot as your spinning knee locks. Keep your free leg stretched, with your toe turned out. Round your arms slightly and pull your shoulders back as your leg lifts. Hold this position and stretch your body over the ball of the foot to increase your speed. To exit, bring your body upright, bend your knees, and push out away from the spin. Hold and stretch the exit position of this spin.

Camel Spin—Darby Gaynor
©David Madison 1998

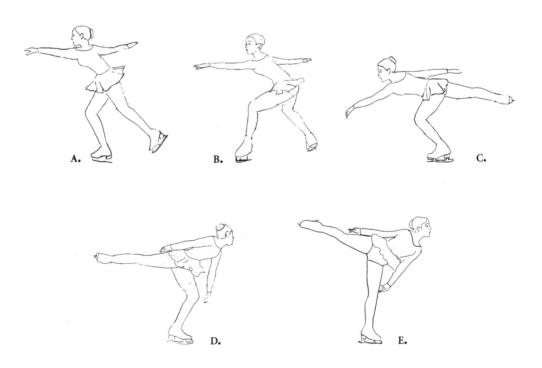

Layback Spin

(**A, B**) The layback spin begins with the same entry as the scratch spin. (**C**) Once you have centered the spin on top of the three turn in the upright position, with your arms and free leg extended out and lifted, (**D**) assume the attitude position as you stretch and lay back, lifting your arms up from the extended position toward the ceiling. (**E**) Round your arms and lift your hands over the line of your chest. Keep your free knee lifted in the attitude position, with the line of the foot and the free knee at the same level.

(**F**) Press into the ball of the foot, keeping the hips under and in line with the spinning foot. Keep your position still. Let your head and shoulders pull back toward the ice as you stretch your hands up toward the ceiling while rounding your arms directly over your chest. Remember to keep your thighs and knees apart while in position and your free toe turned out and pointed.

To exit the spin, come upright with your body tall. Bend your knees with your feet together and push away from the spin on the back outside edge. Hold the exit position on the back outside edge.

Layback Spin—Linda Park
©David Madison 1998

A.   B.   C.

D.   E.   F.

Layback Variation
Blade Spin

(C) Use the same entry as for the layback spin. (E) Attain the layback position. Bring your free hand to the blade of your free foot. Grab the blade from the outside with your palm up in between the sole and the blade. (F) Bring the blade to your head while maintaining the layback position. Lift your elbow to the side of your face. Lengthen and stretch your free arm straight up toward the ceiling. Press on the ball of your foot, and hold this position.

To exit, release your hand from the blade. Return upright, and push out and away from the spin. Hold your exit position.

Note: Pushing into the spin creates more force and allows for a faster spin.

Layback Variation Blade Spin—Rebecca Erb
©David Madison 1998

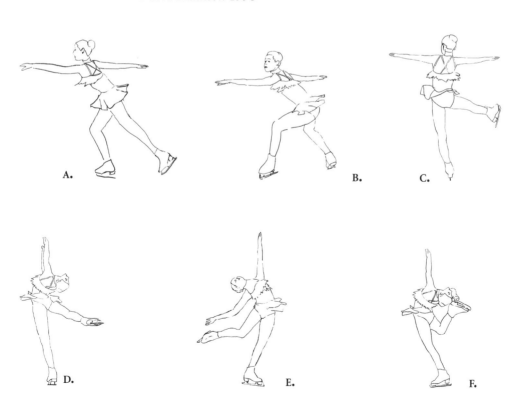

BEILLMANN SPIN

(C) Use the same entry as the scratch spin. Keep your body position upright as you look back at and reach for your blade. (D) Grab the blade with your free hand, palm up, and pull it up behind your head. (E) Reach back behind your head with your other hand and grab the blade. (F) Holding the blade with both hands, bring your upper body forward. (G) Extending both of your elbows allows your free leg to lift higher. (H) Lay your head back to reach maximum extension. Keep the pressure on the ball of your foot. To exit, release your hands from the blade and return to the upright position, then bend and push out of the spin. Stretch and hold your exit position.

Beillmann Spin—Linda Park
©David Madison 1998

A.   B.   C.   D.

E.   F.   G.   H.

Sit Change Sit Spin

You enter this spin using the same entry as the sit spin. (F) From the sit position, (G) open your arms and then take a quick wide push to change feet and begin the back sit. Stay down in your knees and directly over of the center point of the forward sit. As the inside edge widens from the push, place your free toe down, turned in and backwards to achieve the back sit position, (H) press down into the ball of your spinning foot while pulling in your pushing leg and your arms. Keep your head straight, your chin up, your shoulders down, your chest lifted, and your back straight. Keep your free leg stretched and your toe turned out and pointed.

To exit, push up to the upright backspin position, with your free leg and your arms extended. Bend your skating knee and stretch your free leg straight back over the back outside edge. Hold this exit position.

Sit Change Sit Spin—Linda Park
©David Madison 1998

A.

B.

C.

D.

E.

F.

G.

H.

I.

Camel Sit Change Sit Combination Spin

(A, B) The entry is the same as for the camel spin. (D) From the camel position, (E) bring your free leg around and your arms forward simultaneously into the sit position. (G) Keep your head up and quickly assume the sit position. Press on the ball of your foot and hold a tight position. (H) To change from the sit position, open your arms, stay down low, and push into a back sit. After the push, (I) close your arms and pull your free leg into the back sit position.

(J) Press on the ball of your foot and stretch in this position, with your shoulders down, your chest lifted, and your head up. Your free leg should be stretched and turned out, with the free toe pointed. To exit, push up to the back upright position, with your arms stretched out and your free leg back, stretching it over the outside edge. Bend your skating knee as your free leg extends back. Stretch and hold your check position when you exit.

Camel Sit Change Sit Combination Spin—Linda Park
©David Madison 1998

CAMEL CHANGE CAMEL SPIN

(A) Using the same entry as for the camel, hold the camel spin position with your arms extended. (B) To make the change, bend your spinning knee and push into the back camel. As you make the change, stay down in your knees and the back inside edge will widen from the push. Place your toe down on top of the center point of the camel spin and press down into the ball of your foot.

(C) Quickly lift the pushing leg straight back behind the hip into the back camel position. Keep the knee of your free leg stretched and locked, with your toe turned out and pointed. (D) Rise up on your spinning knee, pressing down into the ball of your foot.

(E) Hold this position, with your chin up and your shoulders back. Your free leg should remain lifted and stretched in a still position.

To exit, bring your body upright, with your free leg forward and your arms extended. Then exit onto the back outside edge, with your free leg moving quickly to the back. Bend your skating knee and stretch your free leg back over the outside edge. Hold this exit position.

Camel Change Camel Spin—Darby Gaynor
©David Madison 1998

A.

B.

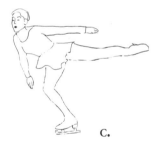

C.

D.

E.

Camel Change Camel Back Sit Spin

(A) This spin is the same as described in the camel change camel with the following additions. (E) From the back camel position, pressing on the ball of the foot, (F) bend your skating knee and bring both arms and your free leg forward into the back sit position. Keep your head up and chest lifted with your free leg stretched and your toe turned out and pointed. Hold this position tight and still, with your weight pressing down into the ball of your foot for a centered and fast spin.

To exit, push up into the upright position with your arms out and your free leg extended. Exit this spin on the back outside edge into the check position. Hold and stretch in this final position.

Camel Change Camel Back Sit Spin—Benny Wu
©*David Madison 1998*

A.

B.

C.

D.

E.

F.

Camel Jump Camel Spin

I have described this spin in a counter clockwise direction in order to provide more detailed instruction. Use the same entry as described earlier for the camel spin. (**A**) From the camel spin, in preparation for the jump, bend your spinning knee and look to the left with your chin up. Keep your arms out, and your chest open and forward.

(**C**) The jump begins with a quick push out of the knee and lift off your toe pick. The free side and right leg swing around in a circular motion, jumping up and around, and landing on the right toe and pressing down onto the ball of the foot. (**D**) The left leg lifts up into the back camel position from the push off of the toe. (**E**) Bend the right knee slightly on the landing of the back camel as your head checks to the right. (**F**) Then push up out of the spinning knee, with your free leg lifted and pulled back behind the free hip and in line with your head. Extend through both knees with your free foot turned out and pointed. Stretch in the camel position, holding your body tight and still while pressing down into the ball of the foot for a fast spin.

On this spin, any unnecessary movement will result in significant loss of speed and balance. To exit the spin, assume the backward upright spin position and exit onto the backward outside edge. Stretch and hold the final checked position.

Camel Jump Camel Spin—Rebecca Erb
©David Madison 1998

A.   B.   C.

D.   E.   F.

Flying Camel Spin

(**B**) The spin begins from a forward outside edge with a deep knee bend. (**C**) Bring your upper body forward with your chest aligned over the skating knee and forward outside edge. Keep your chin up as your pushing leg (free leg) extends back. Pull the leading arm all the way back, inside of the entry edge, while pressing down into the ball of the foot on the forward outside edge.

As its curve tightens, the edge comes around to the toe. Remain forward on the outside edge on the jump takeoff. (**D**) The free side and leg come around in a circular motion, and the jump occurs with a quick push out of the knee and up off the toe. Jump up and over the take-off edge while achieving the flying position in the air.

(**E**) It is important that you assume the flying position and are not just stepping over into the back camel position. Getting into the flying position helps you avoid any unnecessary deductions from the judges during competitions.

The landing from the flying position into the back camel spin is to the outside and crosses over the take-off edge. Land on your toe, with the spinning knee bent. (**F**) Push up out of the spinning knee while pressing into the ball of your foot, and keep your free leg extended and lifted behind the hip, and your toe turned out. (**G**) Stretch and hold the camel spin position still and tight.

To exit, assume the backward upright spin position and exit onto the back outside edge. Check and hold your stretch in this final position.

Take off and landing in the clockwise

and counter clockwise directions.

Flying Camel Spin—Rebecca Erb
©David Madison 1998

A.

B.

C.

D.

E.

F.

G.

FlyiNq SiT SpiN

Enter this spin from a back crossover. From the back inside edge, stretch your free leg under your supporting leg. Rotate your upper body into the curve. Push forward at the top of the circle onto the forward outside edge, staying down in the knee bend.

(A) Bring both your arms back with the free leg. Press down from the knee bend into the ball of your foot. (B) Swing your arms and free leg up and lift into the flying sit position as your skating foot pushes up from your toe and then extends for maximum lift. (C) Quickly tuck your jumping leg up and stretch your free leg with the toe turned out to achieve the flying position. The position of the free leg should be open.

To land, stretch your jumping leg down from the tuck position. Land on your toe. (E) To assume the sit position, press down on the ball of the foot and sit quickly while pulling your free leg into the sit position. Keep your head up and hold this position still and tight. To exit, come upright and open your arms. Bend your knees and push out away from the spin. Hold this exit position.

Flying Sit Spin—Whitney Gaynor
©David Madison 1998

Flying Change Foot Sit Spin

The entry for this spin is the same as the flying sit spin. (C) Push up into the flying sit spin position. (D) At the peak of the jump, the position changes into the reverse tuck when you extend your tucked leg forward while tucking the extended leg back into the reverse flying sit spin position. To land, stretch your leg down from the tuck position, landing on your toe.

Press down into the ball of your foot and assume the back sit position quickly. Hold the position of the back sit, stretching and remaining tight. To exit, push up into the back upright position.

Exit onto your back outside edge. Stretch and hold the exit edge.

Flying Change Foot Sit Spin—Whitney Gaynor
©David Madison 1998

DEATH DROP SPIN

This spin is most commonly seen off the question mark entry from backward cross-overs. From the final stretch position of the back inside edge, push forward onto the outside edge bringing both arms back with the free leg and pressing down into the skating knee. Bend as if you were going to take off for an open Axel.

(A) Allow the jump to travel up into the air with your arms and free leg leading, bringing it up and around. Push up from the jumping leg and stretch it back, with your arms extended in opposition as your leg lifts behind into full extension. (D) Bring your upper body forward to achieve the position of the layout at the top of the jump. (E) Keep your chin up.

To land, stretch your front leg down under your hip, landing on your toe. (H) Your free leg and arms must quickly pull into the back sit position while you press into the ball of the foot. The free leg should not tap or touch the ice, actions that will result in deductions from judges during competitions. To exit this spin, push up out of the back sit position into the back upright, and exit onto the back outside edge. Hold this position.

Death Drop Spin—Chris Conte
©David Madison 1998

Chapter Eight
Get Yourself Airborne—
Learning the Jumps

Tracy: No two skaters execute an element in exactly the same way. Timing in the execution of jumps varies because of factors like your size and body type, and your skating speed going into the jump. In this chapter, I give you precise instructions on the placement of patterns for jump setups, as well as general timing tips for each of the single jumps. Then I provide the additional information about the double and triple jumps. I feel you must build a solid foundation from a *correct* single jump before mastering the doubles and triples. The numbers that refer to the Timing Tips are plotted on the diagram of the rink for each jump.

WALTZ JUMP

The pattern I like to incorporate into the waltz jump is the same for the Axel and double Axel. Starting from fast forward crossovers around the end of the rink, begin stroking down the side close to the barrier in a large open pattern. Take a right inside Mohawk (facing into the curve) as you approach the second blue line. From the Mohawk, push backwards from the left back inside edge over onto the right back outside edge.

Rotate your head, upper body, and free leg back in alignment over the edge while gliding across the arc. Maintain a vertical axis over the skating right foot. Your position over the outside edge should be tall and still as you approach the top of the arc. Move your arms in front of your hips while you prepare to push onto the forward outside edge.

Your free foot should draw into the pushing right foot and directly under the hip in order to have your weight centered and your takeoff edge controlled on the push forward. Bend and push onto the left outside edge over the arc in the direction of travel as you extend both arms and the free right leg behind. (A) Keep your free leg low to the ice with the free right side stretched back. Keep your head straight, chin up, shoulders back and in line with your hips, and keep your chest out and lifted over a deep knee bend on the take-off edge. Press down into the ice over the ball of the foot as the arms and free foot pass through. (B) Push up off the left toe and extend through the jumping leg. Move your arms through in an under and up motion. The arms and free leg are timed with the jumping action from the release off the toe.

(C) The free right leg will lift up high and extended, leading up to the top or peak of the jump. As you travel forward across the arc, (D) your legs should be in a split and open position with your weight shifting over onto your landing right leg to rotate the one-half revolution and descend from the air preparing for the landing.

Stretch the landing right leg and toe under your hip, keeping your hips pushed forward, your back straight, your head up, and your arms extended out. The landing should be soft and light over the right toe. Then shift to the ball of your foot with your skating knee deeply bent over the right back outside edge. At the same time your free leg passes quickly to the back behind the landing foot and lifts straight up over the outside edge in a stretched position. Your free knee should be locked, and your toe turned out and pointed. Your head and the chin should be lifted and in line with the back outside edge. (F) Stretch and hold the landing position.

E.

F.

TIMING TIPS

Count #1 Push onto the (right) back outside edge from the Mohawk.

Count #2 Stretch on the back outside edge.

Count #3 Push and stretch onto the forward outside edge.

Count #4 Jump up!

Waltz Jump—Rebecca Erb
©David Madison 1998

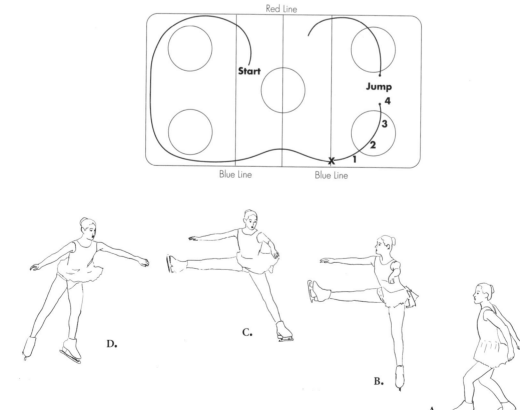

SINGLE SALCHOW JUMP

The pattern I incorporate for the Salchow is almost the same as for the waltz jump, Axel and double Axel. This pattern remains the same for the double and triple Salchow.

Begin by skating fast forward crossovers across the end of the rink and then stroking on forward inside edges down the side close to the barrier in a large, open pattern. Skate the inside Mohawk facing into the curve as you approach the second blue line. From the Mohawk, push backwards from the left back inside edge over onto the right back outside edge. Then rotate your head, upper body, and free leg back in alignment over the right back outside edge while gliding across the arc, maintaining a vertical axis over the skating right foot.

The position on the outside edge should be tall and still while you prepare to push forward onto the left forward outside edge. Your free left foot should draw into the pushing foot and directly under the left hip to have your weight centered on the push forward. (**A**) Bend and push onto the left forward outside edge over the arc in the direction of travel, extending your pushing leg back behind and squaring off your shoulders to the forward left outside edge.

Look straight ahead in the direction you are traveling, with your hips under and free right leg stretched back. Take the three turn across the top of the arc, turning on the long axis. (**B**) Keep your free right leg stretched and low, and extended back over the back inside edge. Stretch your arms out at chest level to create resistance, with your shoulders remaining level and checked directly over your hips. Maintain the vertical axis over your skating left foot.

Stretch your free or right side back over the edge, while looking in the direction from which you have come, and stay aligned over the front of your skating left foot. These two points must stay in alignment to maintain a vertical centered position on takeoff. (**C**) Bend deeply into the skating knee as you move your free right leg and right foot to the inside of the curve, following the back inside edge around to the point of takeoff.

(**D**) Push up off the toe, and extend through the jumping leg. The arms and free leg are timed with the jumping action from the release off the toe. (**E**) Your free leg lifts up high, extending to the top of the jump. As you travel forward across the arc, your legs should be in a split and open position with your weight shifting over at the top to the leading right leg to rotate the one-half revolution. Descend from the air over your landing leg.

F.

E.

G.

D.

(**F**) To prepare for the landing, stretch the landing right leg and toe under the hip. With your hips under and your back straight, extend your arms out, keeping your head up. The landing should be soft and light over the toe, with your knee absorbing the impact.

Press down into the ball of your foot over the back outside edge and bend your skating knee forward over the edge. Your free left leg passes quickly behind your landing foot and lifts straight up over the back outside edge in a checked position with your arms stretched, your free leg lengthened, and your foot turned out and pointed. Your head and chin lift up over the back outside edge. (**G**) Stretch and hold this position.

Single Salchow Jump—Rebecca Erb
©David Madison 1998

TIMING TIPS

Count #1 Push and stretch on the forward outside edge.

Count #2 Stretch back (after three turn) on back inside edge.

Count #3 Bend skating knee, bring the back inside edge around with your free leg inside the curve, push up to the toe pick, and step through lifting up forward.

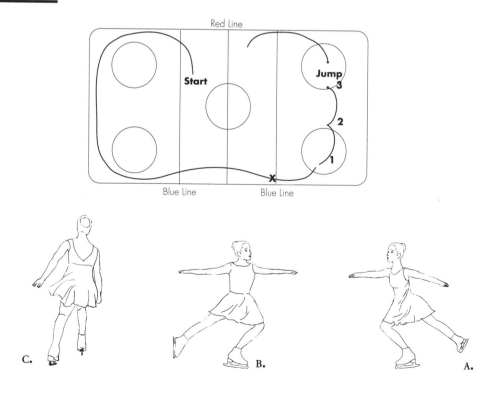

SINGLE TOE LOOP JUMP

The approach I like to use for the toe loop—the question mark pattern—is also used for the single, double, and triple toe loop, and the single, double, and triple flip. With skaters who are very comfortable with it and are consistent with the timing of their edge jumps, I often incorporate that pattern for the Axel, double Axel, double Salchow, and triple Salchow.

The question mark pattern begins with fast backward crossovers. (My example is for skaters jumping to the left. Reverse directions for skaters jumping to the right.) Skate right over left back crossovers around the end of the rink with your arms stretched out straight and with your chin up, looking in the direction of travel. Finish the rounded curve of the question mark while gliding on the right back inside edge. Stay down in your knee bend, and push forward from the right back inside edge onto the left forward outside edge by extending your pushing leg back while bringing your free foot through under your hip in the direction of travel. Place your foot down on the left forward outside edge.

Skate one forward crossover, right over left, as you approach the first blue line. From the right forward inside edge, with your free foot extended under, bring your extended free left leg through by bending the knees and passing your free foot directly under the left hip with your feet close together at the heels.

Push from the right forward inside edge onto the left forward inside edge as you approach the red line. Stay down in your knee bend and pass your right foot forward in front of the left forward inside edge, with your free leg stretched and foot turned out. Looking straight ahead, stand tall with your hips under and in alignment with your shoulders. Extend your arms in a straight line with the left arm leading the right arm back, stretching from the crown of the head and staying aligned over the skating foot and the forward inside edge.

Skate forward on a relatively straight path. As you approach the second blue line, move your right arm forward, squaring off over the right hip. Bend and push with your feet close together and, in a good knee bend, skate a left forward inside push onto the right forward inside edge. (A) Extend your left leg back behind the left hip from the push.

Stretch through the three turn, checking your hips and shoulders, and quickly making the turn while maintaining a vertical axis over the skating foot. Keep your head checked over the right side as your right shoulder pulls back. (B) Stretch your arms and deepen your knee bend as your free leg reaches back, your toe stretching low to the ice over the jump axis for the tap.

Move your arms in a down, then up motion, and assist the tap. (C) The timing of the jump action is from the point your toe enters the ice backwards. Your hips and shoulders rotate

D.

E.

F.

together as the right back outside edge pulls through and lifts up, passing the tapping foot and leading up to the peak of the jump as you travel and climb forward.

(**D**) Pull your hands up and out in front of the center of your chest, elbows down. Keep your legs in an open position, with your weight shifting onto the leading right leg for the one-half revolution at the peak of the arc. Keep your hips under and your back straight. (**E**) Stretch your right toe down under the right hip in preparation for landing. With your head up and your arms extended out, land on your toe with a soft knee bend, and then onto the ball of the foot on the right back outside edge. (**F**) Quickly pass your free foot back behind your landing foot, and lift your free leg up into the stretched checked landing position. Hold this landing position.

Single Toe Loop Jump—Darby Gaynor
©David Madison 1998

TIMING TIPS

Count #1 Push and stretch on right forward inside edge before the three turn.
Count #2 After the three turn on right back outside edge stretch.
Count #3 Lift off!

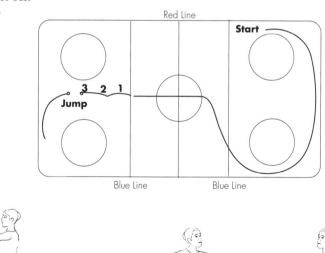

C.

B.

A.

SINGLE LOOP JUMP

The pattern I like to use on the single loop jump is similar to that of the preparation for the waltz jump and the Salchow jump. Begin by skating fast forward crossovers across the end of the rink and stroking with good use of inside edging down the side. Skate a Mohawk at the blue line as you check your shoulders and hips over the back inside edge. Push from the left back inside edge, and step wide onto the right back outside edge.

Maintain a strong check with your right shoulder and hip stretched back. Stretch your arms out over the arc. (A) Pull your left foot across to the inside of the arc, crossing your feet and bending your knees. Press down into the ball of your foot on the back outside edge. Align your head over the front of the right skate, facing straight ahead. (These two points stay in alignment to maintain a vertical and centered takeoff, air position, and landing).

Follow the back outside edge to the point of takeoff and push up off your toe, extending through the jumping leg. Your arms assist the jump in a down, then up motion. (B) Your arms and free leg are timed with the jump action, with your free knee lifting up on takeoff, and your hands pulling through and up in front of your chest in an open position. (C) Travel forward across the top of the arc, (D) rotate one-half revolution, and descend over your right foot.

(E) Stretch your landing leg and toe down under your hip while keeping your hips under and your back straight. Extend your arms out, keeping your head up and checked to the right.

Your landing should be soft and light over your toe, with your knee absorbing the impact on landing. Press down into the ball of your foot over the back outside edge. Quickly pass your free leg behind your landing foot and lift it straight up over the back outside edge. (F) Bend deeply into your skating knee and stretch in the landing position.

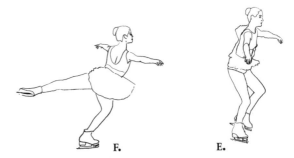

F.   E.

TIMING TIPS

Count #1   Push onto the back outside edge.

Count #2   Bend and grab take-off edge.

Count #3   Jump up off toe on takeoff.

Single Loop Jump—Rebecca Erb
©David Madison 1998

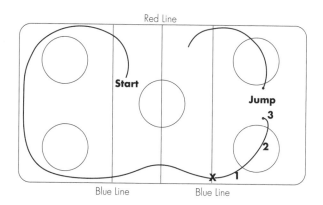

Single Flip Jump

For this jump, use the same question mark pattern as described for the toe loop jump. After skating onto the left forward inside preparation edge with the right foot in front, stand tall over your left skate and extend your arms, with the left arm leading and the right arm back in a level and straight line. Look straight ahead in the direction of travel, which should be a relatively straight path.

As you approach the second blue line, bend your knees and push with the right toe onto the left forward outside edge, squaring off over your left hip. (A) Quickly extend your right leg straight back behind your right hip and stretch your free side back while gliding forward across the ice into the three turn. Lift and stretch through the three turn, checking your shoulders and hips over the left back inside edge. Continue to skate backward in this position on a straight path.

The three turn itself should be executed with a rhythmic timing on the left forward outside and left back inside edges. The distance traveled on the left forward outside edge should be equal to the distance traveled on the left back inside edge prior to take off. The vertical axis remains over your left skating foot. Your head stays straight and checked. Stretch your arms, creating a straight line with the left arm in front and the right arm back, leading over the take-off edge. (B) The skating knee bend deepens as the free leg reaches back with the toe stretching low to the ice and over the jump axis for the tap.

(C) Move your arms in a down, then up motion to assist your jump action from your toe as you glide backward, pushing quickly up off your left knee and right toe on the takeoff. Pull your right arm through as you pull in with your left arm. (D) Your left knee should lift up directly in front of your right leg as you extend it. With your elbows down, pull your hands in to the center of your chest while you climb to the peak of the jump.

Hold your hands in an open position in front of your chest. Keep your shoulders in alignment over your hips. Position your left knee over your right skate. Maintain your legs in an open position but in line over the jump axis (left over right). (E) Rotate across the top of the jump, keeping your hips under and your back straight.

Stretch your right toe down under your right hip in preparation for landing, with your head up and turned to the right. Extend your arms out. (F) Land on your toe with

G.   F.   E.   D.

a soft knee bend, and then let your weight shift to the ball of your foot on the right back outside edge. Quickly pass the free foot back close to the landing foot. Lift your free leg up while extending your left leg back into the checked landing position on the right back outside edge. **(G)** Hold this landing position and stretch!

Single Flip Jump—Rebecca Erb
©David Madison 1998

TIMING TIPS

Count #1   Bend, push and stretch on left forward outside edge.
Count #2   Bend and stretch back on left inside edge (after 3 turn).
Count #3   Jump up!

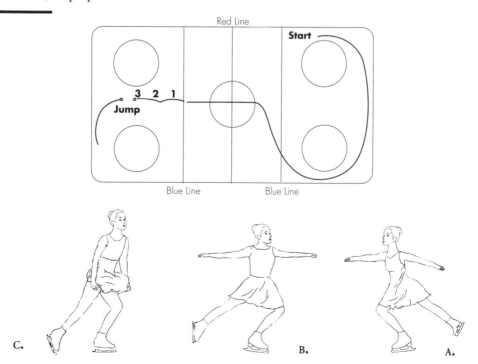

SINGLE LUTZ JUMP

The pattern I most commonly incorporate into the Lutz jump begins from right over left backward crossovers. Skating on a large open circle or curve across the end of the rink and around to the opposite side of the barrier. While executing the back crossovers, stay down in the knee bend while pushing from the edges and extending. Keep the arms up and still. Skate with a strong back, a long neck, and the head looking in the direction you are skating.

Approach the first blue line skating into the curve and completing the back crossover on the right back inside edge. Reach into the curve with the left back inside edge and push onto the right back outside edge while lifting and extending the left leg back. As you approach the red line at the center of the rink, allow the back outside edge to bring the pattern back out to the barrier, creating an hourglass pattern.

Continue to skate right over left backward crossovers on the curve as you pass the second blue line in preparation for the push from the right back inside edge onto the left back outside takeoff edge. From the push over onto the back outside edge, lift your right foot up in front of the skating foot while your head turns from looking in the direction of travel to looking where you have been. The head is lifted and aligned directly over the left skate.

Rotate your head and upper body back over the curved back outside edge. To do this, rotate the head and shoulders while passing your arms through low and close to the body, then stretch your arms out in alignment over the edge, looking in the direction of travel. Check the upper body, still over the edge. Pass your free leg through close to the skating foot, and rotate your head forward, looking in the direction where you have been. (**A**) Continue to stretch the right free leg straight back as the skating knee bend deepens, stretching the toe back low to the ice. Keep your head straight as the arms continue to stretch, creating a straight line with the left arm in front and the right arm back, leading into the takeoff. The direction of travel continues backward on a straight path, with the toe stretching low to the ice and over the jump axis for the tap.

(**B**) The arms work with the timing of the knee bend in a down, then up motion, assisting the jump action from when the toe enters the ice backwards. Pushing up off the left knee, reacting quickly to the toe entering the ice on the jump takeoff; pull your right arm through as your left arm pulls in. Bring your hands together in front of the chest, and simultaneously lift the left knee up directly in front of the right leg as the right leg extends under the right hip on the spring up into the air.

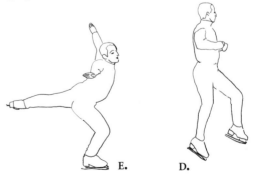

E.   D.

Climb to the peak of the jump with your shoulders and hips remaining in alignment. Your hands should be positioned open from the chest, and touching with the elbows down in position. (**C**) The knee of the free left leg should be lifted, but lined up in front of the right leg and jump axis. The vertical axis is over the right side; the toes should be pointed. The single revolution takes place across the top of the jump. (**D**) With your hips and shoulders in alignment and your straight back, continue to stretch your right toe down under the right hip in preparation for landing. Keep your head up and to the right and extend your arms out. Land on the right toe with a soft knee bend, and then shift to the ball of the foot on the right back outside edge. Simultaneously and quickly pass your left free foot back closely to the landing foot, and lift your free leg up while extending it back into the stretched landing position on the right back outside edge. (**E**) Hold the checked landing position and stretch!

Single Lutz Jump—Chris Conte
©David Madison 1998

TIMING TIPS

Count #1   Push and set position on left back outside edge.

Count #2   The free foot passes through next to the skating foot, and the head rotates forward.

Count #3   The skating knee bend deepens as the free leg and toe extend back for the tap.

Count #4   Jump up!

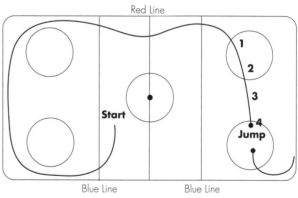

C.

B.

A.

Single Axel Jump

Start with the same pattern as for the waltz jump. (**A**) Push onto the left forward outside edge, pressing down into your knee bend with your arms and your free leg extended back, and the right side of your body stretching back as your skating side leads on the take-off edge. Keep your head up and your chest out over a deep knee bend, with your hips tucked under and in alignment with your shoulders and with your free knee bent. Stretch with the toe of your free foot back behind and close to the ice.

With your head straight and your chin up, look in the direction of travel as you prepare for the takeoff. Pressing down into your knee bend and the ball of your skating foot, pass your arms and free right foot through as you lift your free knee up, pushing off your toe and extending through the jumping leg. (**B**) Move your arms simultaneously with your free leg and time the jump action with the push up off the toe. Now you are traveling forward into the air as you step up to the peak of the jump.

Pull your hands in to meet in front of your chest with the elbows down. (**C**) Step down onto the right foot, pulling the left foot (from the push upwards on takeoff) over and lift your left knee directly in front of and in line with your right leg. Extend your right leg in the air position with the toes pointed. Keep your legs in an open rotating position aligned over the axis, with your left knee lifted and lined up over the right skate.

Your left hip is lifted, closed, and forward for centered rotation over the right side. Rotate one and one-half turns across the arc for the landing, keeping your head up, your back straight, and your hips under you and in line with your shoulders. (**D**) Open your arms and check your head and shoulders into the curve to stop the rotation. Land on your right toe with a soft knee action and then on the ball of your foot on the right back outside edge. (**E**) Quickly and simultaneously, pass your free foot back close to your landing foot, and lift your free leg while extending it back into the checked landing position. (**F**) Hold your landing position and stretch.

F.

E.

TIMING TIPS

Count #1   Push onto the (right) back outside edge from the Mohawk.

Count #2   Stretch on the back outside edge.

Count #3   Push and stretch onto the forward outside edge.

Count #4   Jump up!

Single Axel Jump—Rebecca Erb
©David Madison 1998

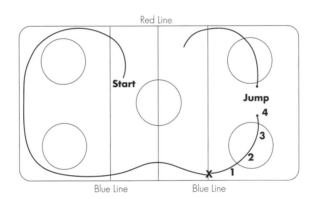

Double Salchow Jump

The double Salchow is based on the same pattern and timing as the single Salchow. (**A**) From the bend, push forward onto the left forward outside edge in the direction of travel, and extend your pushing right leg behind your skating left foot. Square your shoulders parallel to your hips and maintain a vertical axis over your left foot.

Skate the three turn across the arc, turning on the long axis and checking the free right side back. Keep your free right foot low and stretched behind over the back inside edge. Stretch your arms straight out at waist level to create resistance, with your shoulders remaining level and checking directly over your hips and left back inside edge.

(**B**) Maintain the vertical axis over the skating left foot, looking in the direction from which you came with your head facing and aligned over the front of your left skate. These two points must be aligned for a centered takeoff.

Bend deeply into your knee bend as your free foot and leg move to the inside of the curve. (**C**) Now follow the back inside edge around to the point of takeoff. (**D**) Push up off your toe and extend through the jumping leg, stepping through and up forward over the arc. With your right foot leading on takeoff, the right side passes through simultaneously in a down, then up motion. Pull your hands in to meet at the center of your chest, with your elbows down in the rotating position.

(**E**) Step down onto your right foot and cross your ankles left over right, with your toes pointed and your legs stretched in the rotating position and your left hip closed, lifted and forward. (**F**) Rotate the one and one-half revolutions across the arc of the jump with the first one-half revolution of the jump occurring from the back inside edge off your toe to the lifting through forward on the takeoff. As you descend, keep your head up, with your right toe stretched under your hip in preparation for the landing and with your hips under and back straight.

(**G**) Open your arms, and uncross your left foot by lifting your left knee up. Check your head and shoulders into the curve to the right as your right toe hits the ice with your landing knee bent. (**H**) Stretch your arms, and quickly pass your free foot back close to your landing foot. (**I**) Extend and lift your free leg back over the outside edge in the checked landing position. Hold and stretch this landing.

TIMING TIPS

Count #1 Push and stretch on the front outside edge.

Count #2 Stretch back (after the three turn) on the back inside edge.

Count #3 Bend skating knee, bring the back inside edge around with free leg inside the curve push up off the toe pick and step up forward.

Double Salchow Jump—Rebecca Erb
©David Madison 1998

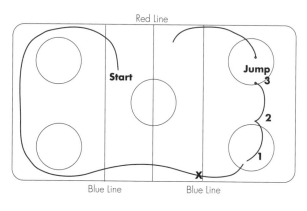

D.   C.   B.   A.

Double Toe Loop Jump

(A) From the push into the three turn onto the right forward inside edge, bend your skating knee as your free leg extends straight back. Stretch your free leg through the turn checking your shoulders and hips, maintaining a vertical axis over the skating foot. Your head stays checked over your right side as your right shoulder pulls back.

(B) Stretch your arms and deepen your knee bend as your free leg reaches back with your toe stretching low to the ice over the jump axis in preparation for the tap. The distance traveled on the forward inside edge prior to turning the three turn should be equal to the distance traveled on the back outside edge prior to the takeoff.

Move your arms through in a down, then up motion and assist the tap, timing the jump action from the point the toe enters the ice backward. (C) Your hips and shoulders rotate together as the right back outside edge and foot pulls through and lifts up, passing the toe on the tap and leading into the air while you travel and climb forward. Pull your hands up and out in front of you directly into the center of your chest, with your elbows down in the rotating position.

(D) Step onto the leading leg (right) and extend it down under your right hip, pulling the left foot in front, and crossing the ankles left over right. The weight will transfer onto your right side to rotate the remaining one and one-half revolutions across the peak of the arc. (E) The vertical axis is aligned over the right foot and your landing leg.

The position of your free hip in the air should remain closed, forward, and lifted. Stretch your legs and point your toes, keeping your head up, back straight, and hips under.

In preparation for landing, stretch your arms out with your head and shoulders checked to the right and lift your left knee up to uncross your ankles. Land on your toe with a soft knee bend. (G) Quickly pass the foot back, close to your landing foot while stretching it back behind as the weight on your landing foot moves to the ball of your foot and back outside edge. (H) Check your landing position and stretch.

H.   G.   F.   E.

TIMING TIPS

Count #1 Push and stretch on the right forward inside edge before the three turn.

Count #2 After the three turn on the right back outside edge stretch.

Count #3 Lift off!

Double Toe Loop Jump—Darby Gaynor
©David Madison 1998

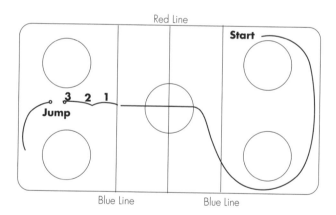

Double Loop Jump

The double loop jump is skated from the same pattern as the single loop. To begin, step wide from the backward push onto the outside edge. Maintain a strong check back with your right side. Your arms should be stretched out over the edge. (A) Pull your left side in front crossing your left foot to the inside of the curve.

While bending your knees, press down into the ball of the foot on the take-off edge. Keep your head aligned over the front of your right skate, facing straight ahead. (B) Follow the curve of the back outside edge to the point of takeoff and push up off your toe, extending through the jumping leg.

Your arms assist the jump in a down, then up motion. Your arms and free leg are timed with the jump action, with your free knee and foot lifting up on takeoff as the right arm pulls through. (C) Pull your hands into the center of your chest, with your elbows down in the rotating position. Travel over the arc into the air with your ankles crossed and toes pointed. (D) Rotate one and one-half revolutions at the top of the arc.

In preparation for landing, maintain the stretch of the right toe under your hip while keeping your head up, back straight, and hips under. (E) Extend your arms out and lift your knee up as your head and shoulders check to the inside of the curve.

Land soft and light over your toe, with your skating knee absorbing the impact. Press down into the ball of the foot over the back outside edge; (F) quickly pass your free foot back behind your landing leg and lift it up while stretching it over the back outside edge. (G) Bend deeply into your skating knee and stretch in this landing position.

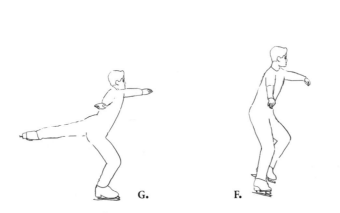

G.   F.   E.

Double Loop Jump—Benny Wu
©David Madison 1998

TIMING TIPS

Count #1 Push onto back edge.
Count #2 Bend and grab take-off
          edge.
Count #3 Jump off toe.

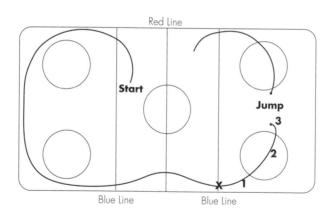

Double Flip Jump

Use the same pattern and entry described for the single flip. (**A**) From the push into the three turn on the left forward outside edge, with right arm forward squaring to the left hip, bend your skating knee and extend the free leg straight back. Stretch your free leg through the turn while checking your shoulders and hips, the head remaining straight and checked over the skating foot. The vertical axis remains over your left skating foot. Your head stays straight and checked. Stretch your arms, creating a straight line with the left arm in front and the right arm back, leading over the take-off edge. The distance traveled on the left forward outside edge should be equal to the distance traveled on the left back inside edge prior to takeoff. (**B**) The skating knee bend deepens as the free leg reaches back with the toe stretching low to the ice and over the jump axis for the tap.

(**C**) Move your arms in a down, then up motion to assist your jump action from your toe entering the ice backward, pushing quickly up off your left knee and right toe on the takeoff. Pull your right arm through as you pull in with your left arm. Your knee should lift up directly in front of your right leg as you extend it. With your elbows down, pull your hands into the center of your chest. (**D**) Cross your ankles left over right with the toes pointed on the climb to the peak of the jump. The left hip is closed, forward and lifted. (**E**) The vertical axis is aligned on the right side. The rotation occurs across the peak of the arc, with your legs stretched and toes pointed, your head up and your back straight and hips under.

In preparation for the landing, stretch your arms out with the head and shoulders checking to the right. Lift your left knee up to uncross the ankles and land on the right toe with a soft knee bend. (**H**) Quickly pass the left foot back close to the landing foot while stretching it back behind as the weight on the landing foot moves to the ball of the foot on the back outside edge. (**I**) Check landing position and stretch.

E. F. G. H. I.

Double Flip Jump—Darby Gaynor
©David Madison 1998

TIMING TIPS

Count #1   Bend, push, and stretch on left forward outside edge.

Count #2   Bend and stretch on left back inside edge after the three turn.

Count #3   Jump up!

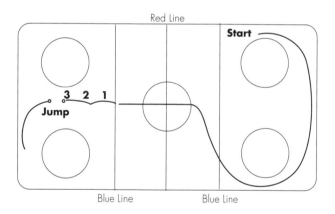

Double Lutz Jump

The pattern for the double Lutz jump is the same as described for the single Lutz. Starting from the left back outside edge, extend your free foot out in front, with your head and upper body rotated back over the outside edge and looking in the direction of travel. Extend your arms out over the back outside edge, with the left arm over the left skating foot and the right arm leading creating a straight line into the takeoff. Keep your shoulders level and checked over the edge.

With your hips under, pass the free foot through beside the skating left foot as your head rotates forward, and looks in the direction where you have been. (A) Continue stretching your free leg and right side back as the skating knee bend deepens on the back outside edge, and stretch your free toe back pointed low to the ice in preparation for the takeoff. The direction of travel continues backward from the arc onto a straight path, and the toe enters the ice in line over the jump axis.

(B) Time the jump action from the point the toe enters the ice backwards. Move your arms in a down, then up motion to assist the jumping knee and tap. Pull your right arm through as the left arm closes in, and pull your left foot back toward the right foot as the jump lifts into the air. (C) Cross your ankles left over right with the toes pointed on the climb to the peak of the jump. Pull your arms straight into the center of the chest, with the elbows down in the rotating position. (D) The left hip should be closed, forward, and lifted. The vertical axis is aligned over the right side.

(E) The double rotation occurs across the peak of the arc, with the legs stretched, the toes pointed together, and the ankles crossed. (F) Keep your head up, back straight, and hips under in preparation for the landing. (G) Lift your left knee up to uncross the ankles, and land on the right toe with a soft knee bend. Stretch your arms out with the head and shoulders checking to the right. Quickly pass your left foot back close to the landing foot while stretching the free leg back behind as the weight on the landing foot moves to the ball of the foot on the back outside edge. (H) Bend your skating knee and stretch in the landing position.

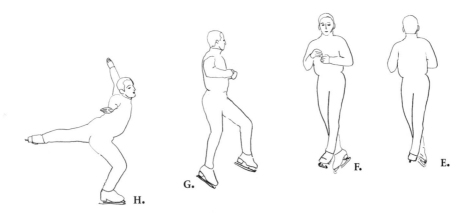

H.   G.   F.   E.

TIMING TIPS

Count #1   Set position on preparation edge.

Count #2   The free foot passes through next to the skating foot and the head rotates forward.

Count #3   The skating knee bend deepens as the free leg and toe extend back for the tap.

Count #4   Spring up!

Double Lutz Jump—Chris Conte
©David Madison 1998

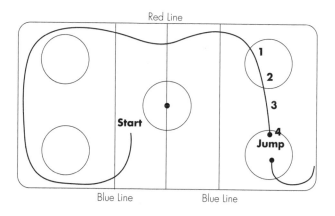

Double Axel Jump

The double Axel builds upon the same pattern and timing as used for the waltz jump and the single Axel jump. (**A**) Push forward onto the left forward outside edge, press down into your knee bend, and extend your arms and your free leg back behind the take-off edge, with your free foot remaining close to the ice. Stretch your arms back with your elbows slightly bent. Keep your chest open and lifted over your knee bend and take-off left foot. Keep your head straight and chin lifted, looking in the direction of travel.

Hold your free side back, with your skating side leading on the left forward outside take-off edge. Staying down in your skating knee with your hips under, press into the ball of your skating foot as your arms and free foot pass through, under, and up. Now push up off your left toe and extend through the jumping leg, timing the jump action from the push off of your toe.

(**B**) Pass your arms through simultaneously with your free leg. Lift your free knee up over the jump axis into a step up position, climbing forward and upward to the top of the jump. (**C**) Pull your hands in to meet in the center of your chest, with your elbows down. Step down onto your right foot, pulling your left foot across over your right foot and crossing your ankles, with your toes pointing down towards the ice. (**E**) Your left hip lifts and is closed and forward in the rotating position, allowing for centered rotation over the vertical axis (right side). Rotate two and one-half turns across the jump arc.

For the landing, keep your head up, your back straight, and your hips under and in line with your shoulders. (**G**) Lift your left knee up to uncross your feet. Open your arms straight out to the side, checking your head and shoulders into the curve and remaining square to your right hip. Land on your right toe with a soft knee action, and (**H**) then on the ball of your foot on the right back outside edge. Simultaneously and quickly pass your free foot back, close to your landing foot, and lift your free leg while extending your left leg back into the landing position. (**I**) Hold the landing position and stretch.

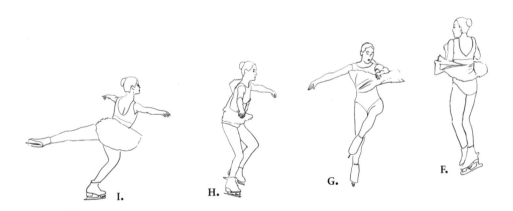

I.   H.   G.   F.

TIMING TIPS

Count #1 Push the right back outside edge from Mohawk.

Count #2 Stretch on the back outside edge.

Count #3 Push and stretch onto the forward outside edge.

Count #4 Jump up!

Double Axel Jump—Rebecca Erb
©David Madison 1998

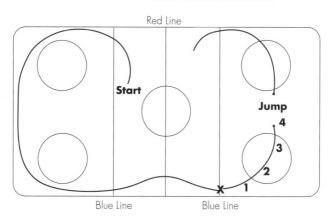

E. D. C. B. A.

Triple Salchow Jump

The triple Salchow is based on the same pattern and timing as the double Salchow. (**A**) From the bend and push forward onto the left outside edge in the direction of travel, extend your pushing right leg back behind your skating foot. Square your shoulders parallel to your hips and maintain a vertical axis over your skating left foot.

Take the three turn quickly across the arc on the long axis while checking the free right side back. Keep your free right foot low and stretched over the back inside edge. Stretch your arms straight out at waist level to create resistance, with your shoulders remaining level and checked directly over your hips and the left back inside edge. (**B**) Maintain the vertical axis over your skating left foot while looking in the direction from which you came. (**C**) Bend down into your skating knee, moving your free foot wide to the inside of the curve, and follow the back inside edge up to the toe. (**D**) Push up off the toe, stepping through forward up over the arc. The free right side passes through simultaneously in a down, then up motion. Pull your hands directly into the center of your chest, with your elbows down in the rotating position.

(**E**) Step down onto the leading right foot (which becomes the landing foot) and cross your ankles with your toes pointed down to the ice. Cross your jumping left leg over in front of your leading right leg to rotate, with your free left hip lifted, closed, and forward in the rotating position.

(**F**) Rotate two and one-half revolutions across the arc of the jump, with the first one-half revolution occurring from the back inside edge off the toe, to the lifting forward on takeoff. As you descend, keep your head up. Stretch your right toe under your hip in preparation for landing, keeping your hips under and your back straight.

(**I**) Open your arms, and uncross your feet by lifting your free left knee up. Check your head and shoulders into the curve as your right toe hits the ice with your skating knee bent. (**J**) Extend your arms and pass your free left foot back quickly, close to your landing right foot. (**K**) Extend and lift the free left leg into the landing position over the right back outside edge, and bend down deeply into your skating knee. Hold this landing position.

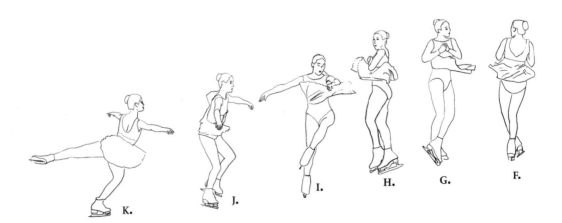

TIMING TIPS

Count #1 Push and stretch on the front outside edge.

Count #2 Stretch back (after the three turn) on back inside edge.

Count #3 Bend the skating knee, bring the back inside edge around with free leg inside the curve, push up to the toe pick, and step through, lifting up forward.

Triple Salchow Jump—Rebecca Erb
©David Madison 1998

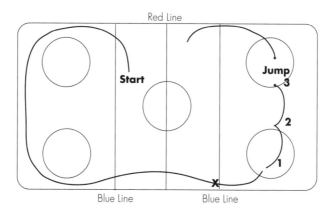

TRIPLE TOE LOOP JUMP

The triple toe loop jump builds upon the same pattern and timing as the double toe jump. (A) From the push into the three turn on the right forward inside edge, bend your skating knee and extend your free leg straight back. Stretch your free leg through the turn. Check your shoulders and hips off a quick three turn, and maintain the vertical axis over the skating foot. Check your head over the right side as your right shoulder stretches back.

(B) Stretch your arms and deepen your knee bend as your free leg reaches back over the jump axis for the tap. Move your arms in a down then up motion to assist the tap, timing the jump action from when the toe enters the ice backwards. (C) Rotate the hips and shoulders together as the right back outside edge pulls through and lifts up, passing the tapping foot and leading up to the peak of the jump, climbing and traveling forwards on takeoff. (D) Pull your hands quickly into the center of the chest, with the elbows down in the rotating position, and step down onto the leading leg, which becomes the landing foot.

(E) Quickly cross your feet left over right tightly at the ankles, and point your toes down to the ice, stretching the rotating position tall and tight. (F) The position of the free hip should be closed, lifted, and forward to maintain centered rotation over the right side. Rotate two and one-half revolutions across the arc of the jump with the first half revolution taking place on liftoff. As you descend from the air, keep your head up and point your landing toe down under the hips. In preparation for landing, with your hips under and your back strong, open your arms, checking the head and shoulders into the curve. Uncross your feet by lifting the free knee up. The toe of the landing foot should hit the ice with the knee bent. (I) Pass your free foot back quickly, close to the landing foot; and lift and extend your free leg back over the edge. (J) Bend down deeply into the skating knee and stretch the landing position out over the back outside edge.

TIMING TIPS

Count #1 Push and stretch on
the right forward
inside edge before
the three turn.

Count #2 After the three turn
on right back
outside edge stretch.

Count #3 Lift off!

Triple Toe Loop Jump—Darby Gaynor
©David Madison 1998

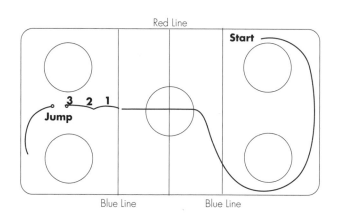

TRIPLE LOOP JUMP

The triple loop jump is skated from the same pattern as the single and double loop jumps. The triple loop jump begins with the back push and wide step into the curve as you maintain a strong check over the right side and back outside edge. Stretch your arms over the arc. Pull your left side in front, crossing your left foot over your right foot to the inside of the arc. (A) While bending your knees, press down into the ball of your foot on the take-off edge. Keep your head aligned over the front of the right skate, facing straight ahead. (B) Follow the curve of the back outside edge to the point of takeoff and push up off your toe, (C) extending through the jumping leg. Your arms assist the take-off in a down, then up motion.

As for all the triple jumps, the reaction time quickens. (D) As you travel in the air up over the arc from takeoff, your hands snap quickly and directly into the center of your chest, with your elbows down in the rotating position and with your ankles crossed and your toes pointed. Stretch on the vertical axis over your right side, (F) rotating tall and tight in position for two and one-half revolutions. The first half revolution takes place on the lift up into the air.

(H) As you descend, keep your head up. Stretch the landing toe under the right hip. Keep your back straight and strong, with your hips under. Open your arms, checking to the right, and check your head and shoulders into the curve. Lift your free knee up to uncross your feet. As you land, your toe should meet the ice with a soft knee bend. (I) Quickly pass your free foot back under the left hip and close to your landing foot, extending and lifting your leg back behind and over the back outside edge. (J) Bend your skating knee out over the back outside edge and stretch in this landing position.

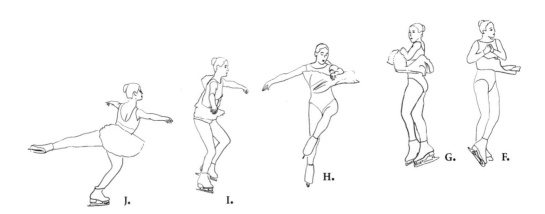

────────

Timing Tips

Count #1 Push onto the back outside edge.
Count #2 Bend and grab the take-off edge.
Count #3 Jump up!

────────

Triple Loop Jump—Rebecca Erb
©David Madison 1998

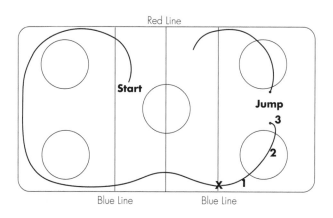

Triple Flip Jump

The triple flip jump builds off the same pattern and timing as the single and double flip jumps. The mechanics of the takeoff should remain true to form, while the reflex action quickens and the rotating position tightens to allow for faster rotation. Both the spring up into the air and the height of the jump are of great importance!

(A) From the push onto the left forward outside three turn, look straight ahead in the direction of travel. Extend your right leg back, and stretch your free leg and right side back through the three turn. Check the shoulder and hips off a quick three turn action. Keep your head straight and checked over the skating side. Maintain a vertical axis over the left skate. The free right side stretches back as the knee bend deepens over the skating side. (B) Stretch your free leg back and reach, with the free toe low to the ice and pointed for the tap. Stretch your arms over the jump axis, with your left arm checked in front of three turn and your right arm stretching back leading into the jump takeoff. The distance traveled on the left forward outside edge should be equal to that of the distance traveled on the left back inside edge prior to the takeoff. (C) Time the jump action from when the toe enters the ice backwards. Push up off the ice (reacting to the toe) with your arms moving in a down then up motion to assist the tap. Spring upwards off the jumping knee into the air. The reaction must be quick and the timing deliberate. Pull your hands straight into the center of the chest, with the elbows down, as your left foot pulls back toward the tapping foot with the toes pointed and the ankles pulling into a tightly crossed left over right position. (F) The rotating position must be tall and tight, with the toes pointed down and the legs stretched. (H) The left hip is closed, forward and lifted, in the rotating position, the hips are under and in line with the shoulders, and the upper body is held still and pulled in tight. Keep your head straight up over the vertical axis on the right foot. This will allow for centered rotation over the right side as you rotate across the arc of the jump.

(I) Descending from the air, keep your head up while the landing toe points down under the right hip. Prepare for landing with the hips under and the back strong. Open your arms, checking the head and shoulders to the right and into the curve. Uncross

H.   G.   F.

I.

J.

K.

your feet by lifting the left knee up. (**J**) The landing toe makes contact with the ice as the skating knee bends. Pass your free foot back quickly close to the landing foot and extend the free leg back over the edge. (**K**) Bend down into the skating knee and stretch the position out over the back outside edge. Hold the landing position.

Triple Flip Jump—Rebecca Erb
©David Madison 1998

TIMING TIPS

Count #1   Bend and push, stretching on left forward outside edge.
Count #2   Bend and stretch on left back inside edge.
Count #3   Jump up !!

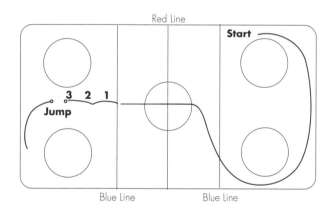

Triple Lutz Jump

The triple Lutz jump builds off the same pattern and timing as the single and double Lutz. A quick push up into the air and achieving maximum height is essential to successfully complete the jump. The reflex action must be quick and the rotating position tight to allow for three revolutions in the air.

From the (left) back outside edge, extend your free foot out in front, with your head and upper body rotated back over the outside edge, looking in the direction of travel. Extend your arms out over the back outside edge, with the left arm aligned over the left skating foot and the right arm stretched back, leading into the takeoff, and creating a straight line.

Keep your shoulders level and checked over the edge, with the hips tucked under. Pass the free foot through beside the skating foot as your head rotates forward, looking in the direction from which you have come. Continue stretching your free leg and right side back as the skating knee bend deepens on the back outside edge. (**A**) Stretch your free toe back pointed low to the ice in preparation for takeoff. The direction of travel continues backward from the arc into a straight path so the toe will enter the ice in line over the jump axis.

(**B**) Time the jump action from when the toe enters the ice backwards. Move your arms in the down then up motion to assist the jumping knee and tap. The reaction must be quick and the timing deliberate! Spring upwards into the air from the jump takeoff, and pull your right arm through as the left arm pulls in. Pull your hands straight into the center of the chest, with the elbows down. (**C**) Pull your left foot back toward the tapping foot, with the toes pointed and the ankles pulling into a tightly crossed left over right position.

(**D**) The position must be tall and tight with the toes pointed down and the legs stretched. In the air, the left hip is forward, lifted, and closed in the rotating position. With your hips under and in line with the shoulders, pull the upper body in tight and still, with the head straight up over the vertical axis on the right foot. This allows for centered rotation over the right side. (**E**) Rotate across the arc of the jump.

(H) Descending from the air, keep your head up while the landing toe points down under your right hip. Prepare for the landing with the hips under and the back straight. (I) Uncross your feet by lifting the left knee up. The landing toe makes contact with the ice as the skating knee bends. Open your arms, checking the head and shoulders to the right and into the curve. Pass your free foot back quickly, close to the landing foot and extend your free leg back over the outside edge. (J) Bend deeply into the skating knee and stretch in the landing position. Hold the landing position.

TIMING TIPS

Count #1   Set position on the preparation edge.
Count #2   The free foot passes through next to the skating foot and the head rotates forward.
Count #3   The skating knee deepens as the free leg and toe extend back for the tap.
Count #4   Spring up!

Triple Lutz Jump—Chris Conte
©David Madison 1998

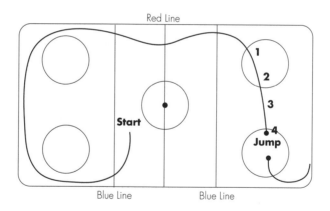

Russian Split Jump

Chris Conte
©David Madison 1998

Butterfly Jump

Chris Conte
©David Madison 1998

STRATEGIES TO HELP YOU
WHEN YOU HAVE DIFFICULTY LANDING A JUMP

Tracy: Working in the harness is a helpful way to get the feel of a jump when you are first learning it. If you are struggling to land a jump that you have been working on for some time, getting back into the harness may assist you in reinforcing the correct feel of the jump. Using the harness can also help anxious skaters practice jumps with less fear about falling and injuring themselves. I am careful not to overuse it, however. I want my students to get the feel of the rotation outside the harness as soon as possible. I also do not want my skaters to feel dependent on it, and be hesitant to go for their jumps without it.

In a lesson, I have my skaters practice their jumps in a sequence from easiest to hardest, and I set limits on the number of attempts that a skater can make with a particular jump during a lesson or practice session. These tips help my students keep the frustration level more manageable. Setting limits on the number of attempts also allows skaters to practice jumps in ways that may prevent injuries to the muscles and tendons from overuse.

Sam: Some skaters like to use key words to describe in an abbreviated form the feeling of a particular jump. They then repeat these key words to themselves as they approach the jump in order to focus their attention on correct execution. Key words can also remind a skater to integrate a certain important correction that the coach has made. Talk with your coach about how this mental training tool might assist you in mastering your jumps more quickly.

Another mental training strategy that you might try when learning jumps is to use optimistic statements to cope with frustration when you are having a difficult time. These statements should tell you what to do (like "pull in") and not what to avoid doing (not "don't fall"). An example of an optimistic statement might be, "each attempt gets me closer to landing this," or "go after it!" These statements are best if you say them to yourself as if you were functioning like your own internal coach, urging yourself to stay with it and to be patient.

Be on the alert for pessimistic thinking when you have worked on a jump for some time and still cannot land it. Quickly turn around any pessimistic thought if you find yourself upset and saying something like, "This jump is just too hard for me. I might as well give up."

Keep yourself hopeful about eventually landing the jump by telling yourself that you *will* get it. It's also important to keep any pessimism about a certain jump from spreading and leading you to think you can't do other jumps well, either. Use a success review to remind yourself of the things that you are doing well in your training. Be certain to end each practice or lesson on a successful note by finishing with an element or move that you do very well.

Refer back to chapter three and remember the hazards of over-personalizing the difficulty you are having with a particular jump. For example, you might be hearing yourself say, "I can't land it at all. It means I can't skate. Maybe I should give up." Keep your perspective. Jumps like the Axel are challenging for most skaters. Some people may take months or even years to master the double Axel. Remind yourself to be patient with your progress. Talk to high-level skaters who are truthful about the long process they went through to reach their goals.

Also keep in mind that jumps may be even harder for you if you are truly experiencing an off day, whether it's because you are tired, getting sick, haven't eaten much, or have been overtraining and are really physically fatigued.

Part Four

Skating Well at Competitions and on Test Days

Chapter Nine
Developing Outstanding Programs

THE INITIAL STEP—SELECTING THE MUSIC

Tracy: Programs are the heart of competitive skating, the product that a skater or team works on all year long. For professional skaters, programs are the core of their performances for the ice shows, showcases, and pro competitions that have become very popular. For a skater who skates recreationally, he or she may want to put together elements and artistic details for the pure enjoyment of creating something like a program.

How is a program created? As a coach, bits and pieces of a program for a particular student come to mind when I'm driving or relaxing. I'll find myself listening to music in my car or hear something on television, and soon I'm visualizing one of my students moving to this music. Often, my student or his or her parents have heard a musical score that appeals to them, and we talk about the possibility of using it.

When deciding on music, I think of the skater's personality and style of skating. We select music that fits for either a technical or artistic program, but I also think about music that displays the skater's or team's strengths and best elements. The music's tone should fit with the skater's age and level, and I make sure that the skater or team likes the music a lot. Remember how often this music is skated to in a single season!

Because of this, when a student tells me about some music that he or she really likes and can imagine skating to, I pay attention. If a student is too young to know what is needed, or isn't interested in listening to a lot of music, I ask the parents if they have any ideas. I often make the music choices for my youngest students, but I do want to take into account any suggestions from the family, or from other people who have seen this young person skate.

I am well aware that classical music is a good choice as far as the judges are concerned. However, I may also hear something modern and be attracted to that composition. I play it for the skater to get a reaction. Because program music is so often drawn from movies, I'm always looking for something fresh and unusual from other sources. It may be a ballad or an upbeat popular song that's current. Sometimes I gravitate to music that was released several years ago. With classical pieces, I search for something appropriate that hasn't been heard repeatedly at recent competitions.

With the final choice of music made, I listen to it again and again so that I hear the "stand out" points where certain elements or footwork might be placed. A more advanced skater is usually already familiar with the program requirements of the USFSA, but I check the *Rule Book* to be certain I am aware of any changes that might have been approved recently by the ISU and then adopted by the USFSA.

Adult skaters need to check the requirements for their programs, but they also have greater latitude to be original when they create their programs, even using novel props they hold in their hands or incorporating unusual details in their footwork. In the 1997 and 1998 adult national competitions, some of the competitors picked music that is almost never heard in skating. Their choices were welcomed by the judges and seemed to be appreciated by the spectators, too.

The timing of both the short, or technical, program and the long, or artistic, program is crucial. At the upper levels, short programs are two minutes and forty seconds. For lower levels, they are shorter. The long program for a Senior Lady lasts four minutes; for Senior Men and Pairs it is four minutes, thirty seconds. The music must fit exactly, of course, within these time limits, and the elapsed time of a program can be affected by the speed of the playback device. At a major competition, a coach checks with officials in charge of music to make certain that the playback unit speed and the length of the program fit right down to the second. If this is not the case, some adjustment in playback speed might have to be made.

When you start out, a musical composition is often longer than the time allowed for the program. In addition, I don't think I have ever found music that could be used in its original form, that had both slow and fast sections in just the right places. For these reasons, music must be edited, that is, cut up and put back together into a smooth complete package. The final product has the right volume and emphasis—like harp strings being strung or a drum roll played when certain components are skated.

Editing can be done at home if parents have the proper equipment, but most editing is done by specially trained sound people. At the National, World, and the Olympic levels, editing is done in recording studios that charge a high hourly fee. Preparing a compact disc (CD) of a program can cost from $100 to many thousands of dollars to attain the quality demanded in elite amateur competitions. Although some rinks are still using cassette tapes of program music, in the glamorous ice shows, the music and its development are big ticket items for the producers.

MUSICAL INTERPRETATION—GOING FROM NOTES TO MOVES

Tracy: How does a skater go from initially feeling drawn to certain music to finally performing a program at the first qualifying competition? Program development has many parts to it.

Short programs must incorporate required elements yet still be pleasing aesthetically. Long programs let a skater be more interpretive, to weave a story or meaning into the skating. Musical interpretation in figure skating can be helped if a skater is familiar with ballet, modern, jazz, or other dance forms. If the music is a movie score or musical theater selection, interpretation is also enhanced by the skater being drawn into the story it tells. Judges and spectators alike may be familiar with this story as it's conveyed by the music. It's probably rare for the judges or spectators to have actually seen the live Broadway musical or play that is the source of the music, but they may have some idea of the story line.

Some classical program music is taken from well-known ballets or operas. Some memorable programs have been skated by Americans such as Michelle Kwan, who created the Old Testament character of Salome; or Debi Thomas who skated to *Carmen*, or Rudy Galindo, who portrayed the black swan of *Swan Lake* at the 1996 U.S. Nationals.

Many of you have seen on videotape the dramatic interpretation of the classical piece *Bolero* by the British ice dance team of Jayne Torvill and Christopher Dean. Canadian Kurt Browning skated inspired and intriguing programs to music from films like *Casablanca* and *Singing in the Rain.* 1998 Olympic Silver Medalist Elvis Stojko, also of Canada, has consistently chosen music that cleverly suits his athleticism and unique style on the ice.

Most of my students have watched the programs of skaters such as these. I encourage them to take an interest in creating their own interpretation to newer music or to find an original angle when skating to a familiar classical piece. Sometimes a student and I look for a theme or interpretive meaning to make a long program interesting, rather than trying to develop a fully evolved character.

Again, the interpretive aspects must suit the age and level of the singles skater or team. A funny interpretation of a traditional piece can be created if the skater has a fun-loving personality, and can switch competently from serious to humorous expression of the music. One feature that is scored by the judges is originality of the long, or artistic, program so I really stretch my imagination for something new and different.

The rules allow skaters to try out new elements, which is how skating has enjoyed its expansion of technical possibilities. Jumps such as the Salchow, Lutz, and Axel were invented by male skaters Ulrich Salchow, Alois Lutz, and Axel Paulsen. Dorothy Hamill made famous her signature camel, and Swiss skater Denise Biellmann was the first to present, in 1980, the beautiful spin that has her name. Overcoming limits has become commonplace in recent years, beginning with the first quadruple jump, a toe loop, landed by Canadian Kurt Browning in the 1988 Worlds.

In the inventive spirit of these talented skaters, I constantly think about how my students can bring a new look to a spin or spiral, or can approach a jump in an unsual but workable way. I may imagine one of my students creating a distinctive line in a spiral. Footwork is another set of movements where creativity can be demonstrated. Sometimes my more advanced students bring originality to their programs when we think of a different air position for a jump or for the landing in a flying spin. How varied the elements are in the long program is another component the judges evaluate in figuring the marks for artistic merit.

In long programs, it is customary to have "slow" and "fast" sections. This variety helps maintain the spectators' and judges' interest. The slower sections give a skater the chance to catch his breath.

It's obvious to me how helpful ballet training can be in the development of a skater's balance and flexibility, and also in his or her confidence to move gracefully across the ice. Ballet training allows skaters to complete their moves more easily and helps them achieve a refined elegance in their hand, neck, and head positions. I also find that a skater with a classical ballet background already knows the language of choreography.

Sam tells me that there is a concept called the "recency effect" in social psychology. My own experience is that this effect of best remembering what is seen most recently clearly applies to the judges. Therefore, I want a program with a strong finish so that the last impression they have of the skater is really memorable. It's important to have an exciting opening to get the judges attention, a program that keeps the judges' eyes glued to the skater or pair until the music has stopped, and then something they won't forget at the end.

Another important aspect is the strategic planning of the program. What is the skater's most complicated jump combination or most demanding double or triple? I place that jump or combination near the beginning of the program when the skater is full of energy. I consider which direction the skater rotates, as well as any other special technical skills that they may have. In that way we can use them to their best advantage. And certainly the skater's technical goals for the year, like what jumps and spins he or she is focusing on, become the foundation of the technical portion of the program. I want the elements in the program to be challenging enough that the skater can progress in skill acquisition for the season and not become bored.

From my personal best perspective, I don't want my students comparing themselves to other skaters, but I do take seriously the objective comparison of looking at what the technical and artistic parts in winning programs are at my student's level. A student and I often review videotapes of national competitions together to see what won at the top. We then discuss what went into the first and second place programs at last year's qualifying competitions. We stay focused on the objective comparison of elements and moves, rather than on another skater specifically. These objective comparisons give us useful information in building the basics of the program, along with consideration for the rules made by the national and international organizations.

At this point in my career, it is wonderful to have some extremely talented choreographers as a part of our team. I am so fortunate to work year-round with coach and choreographer Louis Vachon. My friend and colleague Chris Conte travels to California two or three times each year to spend several weeks with my students. With figure skating evolving so rapidly as a spectator sport, I think it is in the best interest of a serious skater at the Intermediate level or above to consider the benefits of hiring a professional choreographer.

What exactly do choreographers do? With their background in understanding music, dance, and movement, choreographers have the major task of arranging the required elements, artistic content, and connecting steps to fit the skater's style and integrating the mood and meaning of the music into the package known as a program. If the skater is conveying a story, the choreographer wants to help the skater interpret or translate this tale into the language of skating.

When I first met Louis and Chris, I was immediately impressed with their creative gifts. I also quickly found out how well they interact with other skating professionals and with skaters and their parents. These choreographers made it clear that they work as part of a team that is dedicated to helping skaters reach their highest potential in the sport. Louis and Chris possess extensive knowledge both from working with dance coaches and ballet instructors and from their own formal study. They are experienced professionals who have skated professionally and have performed before large audiences.

In matching one of these professionals to a student, I consider the choreographer's talents and then think about what areas the skater needs to cultivate. For example, a skater may already possess a lyrical style but would benefit from enhancing his quick and snappy moves. That fact would help me determine which choreographer would be the best fit. I also like to use different choreographers for the two programs to add contrast, making it more interesting for the skater and for those who will eventually watch the program. Sometimes more than one choreographer has input on a long program, although one person generally takes charge.

Currently, the way we work as a team is that I hand over the responsibility to the choreographer while I closely monitor the music editing and see that my coaching is building the skater's skills. At all times, there needs to be close communication between the choreographer and me as the programs are taking shape and as we add refinements closer to the dates of the qualifying competitions. With Chris living outside the area, I expect to maintain the choreography for my students after he returns to his home.

Chris Conte: When I first meet a skater, I observe the person moving around on the ice. I notice what the skater does well. When a skater has already picked out music, I ask the skater to just go out and move to the music and ad lib on the ice. This gives me a feel for how the skater's body moves to music. I also try to imagine myself as that skater, feeling the music and interpreting it. This is the beginning of my mental sketch for the program.

I refer to the USFSA *Rule Book* for what must be included in the programs. I find out from Tracy what elements she wants the skater to perform and what entrances she wants for the jumps. We talk about the number of specific jumps and jump combinations and she usually has a pretty good idea where to locate these in the program for the skater's maximum benefit. I also make suggestions for when elements might occur from an overall artistic standpoint and from imagining how the music and elements will fit together, like a jump coming at a crescendo in the music.

In developing the program, I often try to incorporate steps that are comparable to the moves that are required for the next level above their current field level. I use original steps at a higher level of difficulty. For example, with a Novice Man, I'll have him do some moves that are the same level of difficulty for someone in the Junior field. In the short program, each required element is laid out on the ice surface so the judges can easily see it. I don't place any two elements too close together in time, since I don't want the judges' heads to be down making their notes when the skater is skating into a jump. The skater also needs to regroup after one jump before taking off on the next one.

In the long program, I think the same way, but I can experiment more. I leave time for extra rotations, and I can be more relaxed about the how long it typically takes for that particular skater to complete each element.

In my experience, skaters can bring more to the artistic part of their programs when they take an edge class. I find this facilitates skaters being better able to skate connecting steps. Good edges add to the overall presentation quality because skaters are more capable of doing complex movements more quickly.

Skaters lucky enough to take style classes learn several dance forms in a convenient way. I believe all skaters should learn the basics first—what I call "getting the vanilla down and then spicing it." Something like flamenco steps can add sparkle to a program, as do elegant arm positions that come from other dance traditions. I ask a skater to stretch and grow in skating skills in these artistic ways.

By the time I arrive to work with Tracy, she generally gives me the music to start my work. I then educate myself about the music, the composer, the style, and what is unique and special about it. I ask the student how the music is personally meaningful. Often, at higher levels, the student has a long program that tells a story. I ask the student to give me a visual representation of what he or she hears in the music before I start forming the steps. I'm always aware that each movement must match the tempo of the music rhythmically, especially the footwork.

If a student is still deciding about the choice of music and asks for my opinion, I suggest avoiding trendy pieces or the top three pop albums of the year. I also remind skaters that certain classical pieces have been heard repeatedly and probably should be avoided.

Tracy and I always keep in mind the dispositions of the judges. We talk to them at summer competitions on both coasts for their input about what is being put into programs, and we take this feedback into account when thinking about the following year. Tracy and I want judges that we trust to see a skater's program early in the season. We want them to tell us if a program is innovative without being over the top. In our work as a team of coach and choreographer, our goal is to help the skater look as good as possible.

Louis Vachon: After three years of working with Tracy, I started helping students select their music. It can be challenging to find things that the kids like. I also believe that the music and the choreography must match their skating style and personality. Once the music is chosen, I listen to it from the beginning. I start to feel steps as I hear its parts.

For some students' programs, I draw a lot from my dance training, such as when I designed a howdown number for a younger skater, I was able to teach her a number of dance steps that made her program unusual and interesting. Skating is, of course, about movement, so I have to choreograph dance steps with enough movement across the ice. I also have to include all the required elements and compress everything into the time that's allowed.

For other numbers, I draw from the edge-class training that I taught the performers in Ice Capades rather than from my dance background. For slow pieces, I will work out movements that use long edges and beautiful, flowing upper body movements.

I have become known for a slower, more lyrical style. I want my programs to be recognizable, but I don't want to become typecast as a choreographer of slow numbers. I experiment with music like that played in Montreal-based Cirque du Soleil. This sort of music helps create a unique kind of mood and I'll design new moves and steps to go with it, like a flowing move followed by a sudden toe move or stop.

I also want to be innovative by creating moves that are skated in an unusual way, like using the back of the blade for a turn. I stretch my own creativity to generate something eye-catching on the ice. I want to inspire the students I work with in the way I was inspired by the choreographers who taught me so much. When I was with Ice Capades, Nathan Birch and Tim Murphy had a great influence on my growth as a skater. They took me to a higher level of performance, and I hope to do that with the students for whom I choreograph. I have learned from Nathan and Tim how much can be added to a presentation with certain movements of the head or showing a strong back. I want my students to stand out when they compete, in a winning way. I also hope someday these skaters will pass on what I have taught them. I feel inspired as a choreographer by this saying: If dancing is how angels walk, then skating must surely be how angels dance.

Tracy: With all this great choreography, how does a skater learn a new program? I usually teach the program to the skater in pieces, from the beginning, leaving jumps out or using only single jumps. My student is practicing sections of the program while this learning process is taking place. When the skater has a feel for the program in its entirety, from beginning to end, I take the sections apart and polish them. This is when I might change the order of the elements, depending on the skater's response to the whole program. We want the pieces to fit the skater strategically, so that each part can be skated well and skated strong. I might adjust the exact placement of a jump or a demanding spiral sequence so the skater can execute these elements well. A final step in pulling the technical parts together is to have the skater begin to do all the jumps as they are meant to be, as singles, doubles, or triples.

Then I refine the artistic aspects. I may bring the choreographer back in to assist me at this point to get the hand, neck, and head positions just right for the best effect. I may ask the advice of a ballet teacher in making small changes that add to the beauty and sophistication of the skater's program.

In our workbook, *The Skater's Companion,* I share a copy of my timetable for program development for a skating year. To summarize important dates here, most skaters at the Junior or Senior level begin listening to music and thinking about themes for competitive programs soon after U.S. Nationals which are held early in the year. By the beginning of February, I want the music chosen and the editing process to begin. February is also the time when show programs are choreographed and exhibition skating gets underway. March is the primary month for the choreographer's efforts, and April the time for the program adjustments I described earlier. Skaters should be skating run-throughs of their entire programs with single jumps in April.

In May, I have my skaters begin complete run-throughs and I look for any problems that need correcting. This is the month when I start to ask for the judges' opinions regarding the look of the program. I schedule formal critiques in June, the month when many of my students debut their programs in exhibitions. In July, there is usually an opportunity to travel to a serious nonqualifying competition for some practice in front of spectators and judges. Summer invitationals happen in August, and these offer more opportunities for feedback from judges to help with polishing both technical and artistic components.

Program run-throughs increase in number for each practice session through the end of September so that a skater can reach near-maximum aerobic conditioning and become completely familiar with the program. October is an important month in which we aim for that crucial balance between feeling sharp with the program and overtraining. I encourage my students to add some off-ice practice in front of a mirror to their training. This is a strategy for assisting them to see and feel the details of the artistry we want in the program. Videotape review of run-throughs is also helpful during this month, so that everything can be put into place. Skaters need lots of rest, good nutrition, and a well-periodized conditioning regimen during October so they can be approaching the pinnacle of readiness. I take great care to see that students do not peak too early before the Regional competition and arrive there tired or bored.

In November, at Regionals you want a skater ready to be competitive and qualify for Sectionals, but not to be so dazzling that they risk burnout. For elite skaters, the peak should actually occur at U.S. Nationals.

Sam and I have developed a sequence of mental training strategies that correspond to the physical training schedule. These mental training techniques are found throughout this book and in our workbook, *The Skater's Companion*. We want skaters to arrive at Regionals with well-rehearsed mental skills that they have used in practice for focusing and controlling distractions, adjusting energy levels, and managing emotions. Please refer to chapters three, four, ten and eleven for more information about the mental-training side of program development and readiness for competition.

COSTUMES—GETTING SKATERS DRESSED

Tracy: In its simplest explanation, a costume is meant to help bring the skater's program to life, to help create the visual representation of the music. These days in figure skating, costumes are anything but a simple subject. Thousands of dollars are spent on them by World and Olympic contenders, as well as by those going to Nationals. No wonder the mothers of young beginners sometimes fret over the costs of dressing their children for their first competitions.

What's a mother to do? First, it can help to talk with other, more seasoned parents whose children have skated at your child's level. Ask those mothers who made the costumes that look attractive. It may be the mother herself, or she may give you the name of the seamstress who sewed it. Around most rinks, mothers have the names of favorite dressmakers who know how to make great-looking costumes and whose prices aren't through the roof. If you don't like to sew find out who these people are, and be sure to call them early in the season to reserve time for your child.

A skater needs different costumes for the technical and artistic programs. The coach usually has ideas about the look a costume should have in order to compliment the theme and tone of the music selected. Some coaches insist that they take command of costume design. If this is the case, I encourage you to make your opinions known about what color will be flattering to your child's skin tones and eye and hair color, and that you suggest colors that might fit the nature of the music.

Costumes for young skaters should be conservatively cut and not push the limits for being too adult-looking. Although beads and sequins may be popular this year, your child may not like them; and you may truly balk at the price for such extras. They can be expensive.

The ISU and national organizations all over the world, like the USFSA, have developed rules for a costume's appearance. The overall ISU guideline for costumes is that they be "modest, dignified, and appropriate for athletic competition" and not "theatrical in nature." There is also a prohibition against "excessive beading." These rules invite some different interpretations, as you might guess.

There are a few rules that are quite specific, such as the ISU ruling that all ladies must have skirts on the clothing in which they skate. The pant underneath the skirt must be substantial enough that the derrier and hips are covered. Obviously, no high-cut lines are permitted. No one-piece leotards can be worn by women. The midriff must be covered in some way, making for some interesting variations on belly-dance-theme costumes.

For men, the ISU also has issued a few specific rules. The man's costume must have pants that reach the ankles, and the pants cannot be too tight, or be "tights." The man's shirt must have sleeves (no exact length stated), and the chest cannot be exposed with too open a neckline. Again, some varying opinions are probably expressed about men's costumes worn at the elite levels.

I find that my objective comparison plan works for costumes as well as for program design. I have no intention of copying the costume of last year's winner at the Regional or Sectional competitions. However, the student, parents, and I may review what was worn last season and think about what we have liked, disliked, or thought was repetitive, without getting into any specific skater's attributes. I want to keep in mind what judges find pleasing, which I can assume is part of the high artistic marks they gave to a skater in a long program. I also want to keep my student's own style, age, and music theme and character in mind as we join in a team effort to design the costumes.

I am very aware of the financial resources needed for skating, and the sad fact that way too much money can be spent on skating costumes, even by well-meaning parents (and even after I have cautioned that it is not necessary). This is one area where keeping up with the others in the rink can get out of hand in terms of dollars and stress.

I want to be sure that the skater likes the design we are proposing. If he or she doesn't, this can have a negative impact on the good feeling of skating in the costume. And speaking of good feelings, it is important that the skater actually be able to move about in the costume once it's completed. With synthetic fabrics like nylon and spandex, it should be much easier today to make a costume with materials that allow the skater to move freely.

The costume ought to be finished in time for the skater to practice in it for at least two weeks. I know this can't always happen, but it makes me a lot more comfortable to put a skater out on the ice in a costume that feels familiar. Even last-minute sequins make me a little nervous if they could distract the skater because of their newness.

What about hair and make-up for ladies? I think good taste is a helpful guideline here. With make-up, something too theatrical could set off those rule-book alarms. The age and maturity of the skater should be considered in thinking about how much make-up to use. For hair, I mention some safety concerns when I plan the hairstyle with the mothers. The hair should be styled in a way that it doesn't catch in the buttons, snaps, or hooks and eyes on the costume's neckline or elsewhere. If the hair is worn long, any bangs should not get in the way of the skater's view. If ribbons or artificial flowers are worn in the hair, they must be securely fastened and then checked several times to see how well they stay fixed in the right place.

For boys and men, I think the conservative approach is good, meaning hair not too long or cut too trendily. I don't like earrings on male skaters; just a thing with me. I'm not certain where the judges are with this, despite how common earrings are today on the models in men's fashion magazines. Make-up on men may be helpful in the form of a tinted base to brighten up a man's pale complexion, but I don't suggest eye liner or anything else.

A female skater's hands get noticed, and for this reason the nails should be clean and well-groomed. Sometimes my students want to use polish when they perform. We discuss the appropriateness together to decide whether nail polish adds or detracts. The unusual colors that are fashionable in any given year may not appeal to judges. Chances are, a pretty French manicure done at home will be just fine.

Chapter Ten
Getting Physically and Mentally Ready

Sam: When researchers in sport psychology study the best performances of elite athletes (meaning Olympic or professional), they find similarities across sports and nationalities. Terry Orlick (1986) provides a summary of the characteristic behaviors of these athletes before competition and while at the competition site:

They trained hard and well.

They generally entered the event with their own thoughts, feelings, and beliefs on their side (i.e., constructive self-talk, positive feelings, belief in capacity).

Before and during the event, they were free from negative or self-defeating thoughts and were not distracted by high levels of worry. That, in turn, appeared to free their bodies and focus for a peak performance.

They were highly activated before the event but were not feeling extremely anxious or overcome by worry" (p. 25).

How do these actions and mental states apply to you as you prepare for the competition season or for an upcoming test?

First, remember that the best performers in competitions are those who are the best trained. Those who pass their tests have also trained hard, and as a consequence, they are well-prepared to demonstrate their skills for the judges. Planning your training early in the season is crucial. Approaching your lessons and practice sessions with a serious, "I mean business" attitude is also crucial. This is how skaters get to the Olympics.

It is a must to have a program of off-ice training that supports your work at the rink. Being certain that you do your functional stretches faithfully every day helps you attain both beautiful extensions and the flexibility to execute demanding jumps and spins. Eating well, getting enough sleep, and managing your life (all those external distractions) are also important components of your training regimen.

Train with the focus on your own skating and your own progress to prepare you to be focused on your own thoughts, emotions, and plan when you skate at a competition site. Practice your program like you really mean business—skating all the way through with good speed every time. This truly gets you ready to skate well before the judges.

If you learn mental training skills to help you relax, imagine your programs, and turn your pessimism into optimism, you have priceless tools that allow you to deliver your personal best in a competition or on a test day. In addition, practicing to contain your worries before each lesson and practice session gets you so familiar with this technique that you can instantly use it, if you need to, at the competition site.

In this chapter, I teach you how to reach the optimal performance state that allows you to perform your personal best, so that you can be in the "activated but not anxious state" that Terry Orlick describes as characteristic of winning athletes. I also take you through some imaging exercises to mentally rehearse how you want to be at the competition site, before, during, and after your programs.

Let's talk about optimal performance states first. *Intensity* is the term used most recently in sport psychology (Taylor, 1996) to mean the level of physiological arousal—how "up"—an athlete is before and during a competitive event. Athletes experience intensity in different ways. Skaters usually describe it as feeling excited, ready to go, and psyched to get out on the ice and perform. The optimal level of intensity varies from one skater to another.

How can you find this optimal level for yourself?

Think back to a time when you performed your personal best. What did your body feel like? How would you describe your emotional state then? What thoughts did you have? This success review can be the starting point for you to become aware of the level of intensity that allows you to skate your personal best out on the ice.

Too much intensity feels like extreme anxiety or fear, with tight muscles, trembling cold hands and feet, shortness of breath, pounding heart, sweating, and nausea. That level of intensity is over the top, and an athlete cannot focus well because his tense muscles cause him to move stiffly. At its worst, too much intensity results in "choking," in which an athlete literally freezes, can't think clearly, and can't perform. The term *choking* comes from the experience of this near-panic state, and the feeling of choking when breathing becomes erratic.

Although it may seem strange, too little intensity is also a problem. Too little arousal can adversely affect your ability to perform well. Feelings of being bored, indifferent, uninterested, too tired, or ill can become manifest as a state of too little energy to skate your best. The result may be slow speed, lackluster moves, and presentation that looks wooden.

Getting into your optimal state, once you have remembered what it is like, can be tricky without some context in which to recreate it; but if you skate in several nonqualifying competitions, club-sponsored simulations, or exhibitions, you have opportunities to get yourself up to perform before a crowd. If no judges are available, perhaps your coach and a colleague can pretend they are trial judging so you can skate up to this kind of expectation.

In our workbook, *The Skater's Companion*, there are several exercises for relaxing that are good strategies for lowering your level of intensity when it is too high. Here are several techniques for increasing your intensity level if it is below your optimal point.

These are methods I have taught to skaters over the years in summer skating camps, and in sport psychology training sessions, as well as individually to elite competitors.

Using Mental Rehearsal to Prepare for Competitions and Test Days

Mental rehearsal is a powerful tool that you can use in several ways to prepare for competitions and test days. When you are learning a new skill, you can mentally rehearse it before you try it on the ice. For example, you can imagine a jump or a move into a complicated new spin by the boards before you attempt it.

You can also mentally rehearse new skills at night before you go to sleep. If you visualize vividly, see yourself executing the skill properly. If you do not visualize, feel the move or the element as if you were actually doing it. You can also talk yourself through it or say key words to yourself that are helpful.

When you are learning your program, you can listen to your music on a cassette recorder and imagine skating your program to your music. You can also benefit from imagining your program in "real time," without the music, if you have no convenient way to play your music.

Imagining an upcoming competition is another important use of mental rehearsal. In our workbook, *The Skater's Companion*, you can find instructions for getting into a relaxed and comfortable position that is ideal for doing the imagining exercises that are designed for use away from the rink. Here are instructions for exercises that help prepare you mentally for competitions.

First, see if you can imagine the rink in which you will be skating during practice ice. Then imagine the rink in which you will compete, if it is different. This is obviously easier if you have actually been there. Tracy and I recommend that you visit a site, if possible, several weeks before an important qualifying competition.

Imagine skating your practice ice sessions in your practice outfit. Imagine that you feel well-trained, confident, healthy, well-rested and excited about being there. Imagine yourself in your hotel room, feeling comfortable and able to relax and go to sleep when you want to. Imagine yourself at a restaurant ordering healthy food and eating in a calm, pleasant manner. Imagine yourself coping patiently and positively with the long waits, the crowded dressing room, and changes in the schedule.

Imagine yourself being able to find some personal space and quiet time to prepare mentally, away from the noise and confusion of the competition. Imagine that when you feel like you need to be alone, that you say so to the people—usually your parents—you are staying with. Then imagine finding that space and letting yourself unwind.

Imagine yourself warming up before your short program, following the same routine that you use in all your practices. Imagine feeling yourself at your optimal level of performance, ready to step out onto the ice with your group. Imagine yourself on the ice in your warm-up, gliding about confidently, and executing your elements with sureness and quickness.

Imagine yourself waiting your turn to skate, staying warmed up and thinking optimistically about your performance, focusing on what you are going to do on the ice (your performance goal), and chasing from your mind any thoughts about outcomes (like who will win).

Imagine yourself stepping out on the ice, getting into your start position, hearing the first note of your music, and beginning a strong personal best performance. Imagine skating your short program accurately, with graceful artistic presentation and enthusiasm. Feel yourself excited to be doing this.

Now imagine yourself warming up for your long program. Feel yourself ready, excited, full of energy, and alert. Feel yourself being certain that you have all the energy you need to skate this program to a strong finish.

Imagine yourself in your warm-up group, skating with speed and precision, obviously well trained. Feel yourself being excited and ready as you get into your start position. Hear the first note of your music, and then feel yourself skating this program through in real time.

You can follow this same general format for mentally rehearsing your skating on a test day. Imagine yourself arriving at the rink prepared, calm, and ready to demonstrate what you know. Feel yourself waiting calmly for your turn, then imagine skating your skills in front of the judge or judges with precision and confidence.

Another preparation activity for you to discuss with your coach is your set of plans for how you will respond to the unexpected at the competition site. Here is your chance to get creative in thinking of all the unpleasant surprises that can happen to skaters, who often react by falling apart. What you can do to be prepared is to devise a good plan for different scenarios that include thinking optimistically and keeping your behavior and emotions under your control.

On the opposite page is a list of unpleasant surprises that you can plan for and handle well should you need to at the competition. Having such plans does not, by the way, create a self-fulfilling prophecy. Don't worry that because you think of it, it will happen. On the contrary, having these plans means you can now set the worry aside because you have already thought about what you would do if you had to. You don't have to think on your feet.

Add any surprises that you think of to this list, and come up with your best response. You and your coach can arrange to have you practice falling and getting up quickly, or any other of these strategies that it may be helpful to practice.

My Emergency List and Possible Responses

I fall during my program.	I get up quickly, smile, and continue on as if it hadn't happened.
I find my skates missing from my bag.	I use the old, spare pair I brought with me.
The rink is very cold.	I have a sweater, gloves, and other clothes to keep me warm while I wait.
I get hassled by competitors.	I ignore them and focus on my skating. If they are verbally threatening or get physical, I report them to the skating officials.
There are changes in the schedule.	I know to expect them and make mental and physical adjustments so I'm OK.
I am so tired I can't focus.	I find a way to get a ten-minute nap. I use my favorite intensity-increasing exercises to pump myself up.
I break a lace.	I have packed extras, which my parent or coach is carrying.
I tear my leggings or pants.	I have brought extras that I keep in my skate bag.
I collide with another skater and both us of are banged up pretty badly.	I get first aid, calm myself down, see the sports medicine doctor on call and decide what to do. I breathe, stay calm, and keep my perspective. I remember that this is, fortunately, not a life or death matter.

Chapter Eleven
STRATEGIES FOR SKATING
IN COMPETITIONS

Sam: You have arrived at the competition site, checked into your hotel, and checked out the rink. You have figured out the travel time between your hotel and the rink, the best restaurant and the rink, and the grocery store and your hotel.

If you have changed time zones, you get into the routine and behave as if you are already adjusted to the new time. This means that if your new time is noon, you would stay up even though you are tired and in your actual time zone it is much earlier or later.

When you are at the competition site is the very best time for you to be focusing on your personal best goals and thinking about your skating—which is what you can control. Remember, this is the time to stay in the present moment. This is the time to keep focused on performance goals.

Resist the temptation to think about outcome goals. You are well-trained and you have prepared to skate in ways that the judges can give high marks. Ultimately, you do not control who wins. You do not control the conditions at the rink or changes in the schedule. You do not control how your competitors will skate. Your performance goals can help you keep your head together, and they allow you to feel confident and excited.

Write your performance goals on paper and look at them frequently while you wait to skate your short program. An example might be, "I will skate my short with cleanness and sureness. I will go for *everything*!"

If you start to be distracted by competitors, you can use these refocusing internal-coaching statements: "Focus on yourself and your program. Think about what you can control. You are well-trained. You are ready to be here."

If you get distracted by external factors, like the crowd, noise, confusion, bright lights, or a different temperature, use these focusing statements to pull your attention back inside your body.

"Get quiet. Imagine what you are here to do."

"Get into the present moment."

"I feel my feet, my arms, and my hands."

"I feel myself here, right now."

"I can calm myself and stay relaxed and energized enough to skate my personal best."

"I can get into my music and skate to it."

In the section of our workbook, *The Skater's Companion,* that addresses competitions and test days we give you exercises for getting yourself out of the trap of comparing yourself to your competitors. This kind of comparison makes most skaters very anxious. In addition to these methods, you can also find your personal space and begin to imagine skating your program. You can also do something unrelated to skating, like reading a good book, doing your homework, or going shopping!

In our workbook, we give you very specific ideas for eating well, eating healthy snacks, and sleeping well. There are even suggestions for ordering in restaurants.

I want to add a few other ideas here that can help you cope well at competitions. If you enjoy taking walks, find a walking buddy and check with your coach about an appropriate time for this activity. Walking can give you a reprieve from the hustle and bustle of the competition site.

You might also go to a good movie you have been wanting to see, especially a comedy. Make sure that the timing of this does not interfere with your practice ice schedule, any off-ice activities you may be doing, or your sleep.

You can also try to enjoy the company of other skaters whom you did not know before you arrived. Ask them about their lives outside of skating—about their pets, their hobbies, and places they have visited. Practice another kind of focusing by listening intently to what the other person is saying. Share your own stories in kind.

If there is an opportunity for short sightseeing trips, do so if your coach approves. Traveling to a new city for a competition should include time outside the rink to experience different places and people.

Most of all, enjoy yourself as much as you can while at the competition site. Remember that you started skating because you enjoyed it. You have trained hard, and you are serious about your performance goals; but also see if you can have some fun, especially at the competition party if there is one.

STRATEGIES FOR SKATING ON TEST DAYS

Sam: Most skaters anticipating a test day, say that they just want to pass. It is hardly surprising for them to have this outcome goal, but worrying about what will happen if they don't pass can become a problem.

Skaters seem to get nervous about test days for two main reasons—either they are not sufficiently prepared or they are concerned about the consequences of not passing. In this case, they may worry about feeling upset or embarrassed, or be concerned that the judges somehow will think less of them. It may make sense for the coach to postpone the test date in order to allow for more training time and better preparation.

If you feel nervous about skating a test in front of judges, another strategy that may help you is to imagine that you are in a practice session and perceive the judges just as faceless folks out there on the ice. You then skate your very best as you go for elements and show your moves. In this way, you are focusing on what you are there to do, which is a performance goal, and you let go of focusing on being evaluated by others, in this case, judges. This technique has really made a difference for some young people I know, both recreational and competitive skaters.

Chapter Twelve
The Judges Speak

Tracy: Skating, as a judged sport, is unique in its demands on skaters. Skaters must compete by skating programs that conform to the *Rule Book* guidelines for specific elements. Ideally, they should both enjoy their music and choreography and also perform in ways that the audience will enjoy and the judges will view as appropriate for their level and age.

I know it is important for my students to get judges' feedback about their programs before the competition season starts. To do this, I arrange for critiques by judges whose observations I truly respect. For these critiques, the student performs his or her personal best at that point in the training in order for the judge to notice strengths and to point out areas that could be improved.

I help my student prepare to use this feedback in a positive way by explaining how useful it is to have an experienced viewpoint from a person who, as a judge, has evaluated many programs for skaters in the past. Also, I want my students to see judges as human and as people who have a great responsibility when they compare and contrast what skaters present to them at a particular point in time.

For this book, I wanted several judges to talk about their views on the process of judging—how they personally approach this huge task and what it is like for them. I asked them to discuss what they look for as skaters compete. I also asked for their thoughts on what happens when they watch practice sessions at competitions.

Joan Burns is a busy National and International judge who also gives generously of her time and energy both to promoting the sport in general and to making the Peninsula Skating Club a terrific organization for so many skaters, families, and coaches. Rick Perez is a former competitive skater who stays active on the circuit as a National judge. Jon Jackson is a National and International judge who has been a strong supporter of skating excellence. Charlie Cyr is a National and International ice dance judge who brings his caring, warmth, and principles to the judging process.

In the sections below, I describe how they came to be involved in skating and judging and then quote from their conversations with me about the valuable insights and points of view they have gained over the years.

Joan Burns

Joan Burns grew up in San Francisco and skated at a local rink. She recalls that there weren't too many coaches in the area then for experienced skaters. She took lessons with one of them, Hans Johnson, who recommended that she join the St. Moritz Skating Club in Berkeley across the San Francisco Bay.

"My parents," she says "were European. They encouraged me to have outside interests like music. Piano came easily to me, and my parents would have liked me to become a concert pianist. They let me know that skating was my thing, which I needed to do." From age fourteen to fifteen and one half, Joan made the substantial journey to the rink to skate. Her mother didn't drive so Joan got herself up in the morning, took the streetcar across San Francisco, and then rode the train across the bridge to Berkeley to private school and then skating five times each week. "My grades had to be As and Bs," she recalls, "or I wouldn't be allowed to skate."

Then tragedy struck. She contracted polio, a serious crippling disease at the time. After six months in the hospital and twelve months on crutches, she began to get around, painfully; but her skating career was ended for good. "I was devastated by this."

Joan continued her long recuperation. She married and started a family. At one point in the early 1950s she went to Nationals in Los Angeles. "I thought I might like to get back into skating. While there, I ran into a judge who had judged me and we talked." Inspired, Joan began trial judging at the Burlingame Ice Rink which has since closed. (Trial judging is how people get started in judging. They sit with the panel of competition judges and learn the process, but their marks do not count. Competition judges must have first been test judges at the particular level for which they are judging a regional or local competition.)

"The El Camino Skating Club, which was based at this Burlingame rink, merged with the Silver Edge Skating Club in Sunnyvale and the Crystal Springs Club in Belmont to become the Peninsula Skating Club." Joan has been a driving force in building the membership and quality of the Peninsula Skating Club. She served as president from 1968 to 1972, before the club merger, and again from 1996 to 1998. She has worked hard to bring in accomplished skaters and experts in off-ice conditioning, sports medicine, and other fields to help members develop their skating skills and skating wisdom.

Joan, now an experienced National and International judge, comments on the judging process in this way. "In open judging, your mark [one for technical merit and one for presentation] goes up for the skater, independent of the other judges. A lot depends upon skating order, in terms of the final placement. It's hard to do this kind of judging when the skaters are bunched together or are demonstrating similar talent. Experienced skaters like open judging as a rule. Open judging is probably the most accurate; maybe not the fairest, however." In closed judging, the marks do not get displayed until the end of the event. Joan says, "I think that closed judging is better, where marks are always independent of other judges' marks."

These are Joan's feelings about skaters and the competitive process: "I feel coaches need to be honest, sensitive, and tactful [with their students]. Let's achieve these goals of passing these tests while becoming a good human being.

"I don't think coaches should force competitions beyond their skaters' level of talent. Coaches can lose integrity on this.

"A lot of parents don't understand that when their child attempts a jump but doesn't complete the rotation, a judge can't give credit for a cheated jump. For example, a parent or coach can be asserting, 'My skater had doubles and didn't fall,' but this skater may have telescoped the jump or not completed the full revolutions so can't be given credit.

"I look at the overall program and ask, 'who has the better program?' That's my view, but not all other judges might agree with me. Sometimes, because of where they are sitting, judges see from different vantage points. So some of them may see something while another one might not see it and miss it. We judges must evaluate fairly what skaters show us.

"A judge must be accountable. You must have objectivity and not let your feelings, negative or positive, interfere with what you are observing in what skaters show you right then. You have to be very businesslike, almost black and white. You can't let your emotions affect you, for example, when watching a skater from your home club. You must concentrate at all times, so you must be rested and in good shape so you can judge the last skater as well as you judged the first one to skate.

"Judges *have* to know the rules. Yes, sometimes a judge makes a mistake. But that is why there are five, seven, or nine of us on the panel, judging at one time. It's easy to pick out a winner. But it's hard to pick second, third, or fourth place. These places are just as important as the first place.

"Some judges feel the music much better than others. I feel judges should study music and ballet as part of our job of judging. All of us don't always do this.

"I know that many kids and their parents are scared of judges. They shouldn't be. For many years, I have seen this. My advice to skaters is to think about yourself and you'll do better. The minute you think about the judges or other skaters, you aren't focused.

"Judges know that skaters have good days and days when they aren't up. We can't take that into consideration, though. We have to judge what we see at the time. It doesn't matter what club you belong to or who your coach is. *What does matter is what you do when you compete*, not in practice, not in warmup. I'd love to see every skater able to skate every element. The second mark (for presentation) is subjective in judging. But a skater can use that second mark in a constructive way, as a tool to improve yourself."

Joan offers some additional advice. "Judges are looking at the skating first, but a skater also needs to be a complete package. Boots should be clean. A refined, simple costume is fine, one that suits the child's age and features. If a family can't afford a fancy costume, that won't deter the skater from winning."

As a judge who has seen much in her many years of experience, Joan closes with these personal views: "What I hope is, when a skater leaves the sport, that he or she has the right attitude and can deal with emotions, good and bad; that he or she has grown to be a good human being with experiences that can be used later in life."

Rick Perez

Rick Perez is a National judge with a substantial background in skating. In his skating years, 1968 through 1979, he skated both singles and pairs, with Jill Monte. He was coached by Alex McGowan and later by Evy and Mary Scotvold. His pair skating was halted when his partner went off to college. Rick last competed at the 1978 National Championships.

After his father's death everyone in the family had to pull together. Rick had started working nights as a computer operator when his father first became ill. "The financial support for my skating was gone. I didn't compete in singles in 1979 and dropped out of sight in the skating world." He went on to become an operations manager for Hewlett-Packard.

"I had nothing to do with skating until 1984. For Centrals [one of three Regional competitions leading to the Pacific Coast Sectional competition], I was asked to do the announcing because I knew the process. At some point, I was watching the skaters while sitting next to Brian Boitano and skating judge Joan McDonnell. Joan asked me, 'Have you ever considered being a judge? You have the technical knowledge, the temperament for it and the fairness that's needed.'

"That was the first time anyone had suggested it. Later in the season, I was asked to judge a showcase, the Valentine's Jubilee. There, other people talked to me about judging. I thought to myself, I could use what I'd learned and stay involved in skating, something that I'd put a big investment in. It was appealing to stay involved in a small way. So, I looked into the accelerated program where you could work on two levels up at the same time."

Rick trial judged at Nationals from 1993 to 1996. "At Nationals, the chief referee told us, 'Please judge what you see. We will support you in that.'" Rick also notes that at many competitions where he's judged, the best skater there may not have won the event. "It [the judging] is based on what you see that day."

After being a judge for fourteen years now, Rick has several things to say about his experiences. "There are pressures in being a judge. At a qualifying event, you must judge what you see in the competition, not in the practice or even the warm-up. Events occur quickly. You must analyze and place the skater quickly, and be right there. I clear my mind of the skater's history, and count the rotations of spins, the change of foot, the quality of jumps and spins.

"When I'm judging an event, I want to do the best job I can. I get nervous because I want to do a good job. I can't eat. None of us judges wants to do a bad job, especially in open judging when you have to concentrate on your own marks. You must place the skater in your ranking, based on what you see in the event; then you've done a good job. I enjoy judging, even with the challenges.

"So why go to practice? I go to prepare to do a good job. It's too much pressure if I haven't gone to practice and familiarized myself with who's skating. By going to practices, you get to know the kids and who's in what event. You get to know names and get a rough sense of grouping from the practice—this skater is stronger, this skater is somewhere in the middle. But that's all the further I go. What judges are discouraged from doing at practices by the USFSA and the referees is taking notes or talking with one another about the skating. We don't want to give the impression of bias.

"What I like about closed judging is that all through the event, I can make adjustments. In open judging, all decisions are final after each skater, with no safety net. I remind myself that I am one of five, seven, or nine judges. My part is to put my ordinals in there where I think the skaters should be. I'm aware of all the time skaters devote to skating and the money their parents put into it, and the coaches' efforts. I feel that as long as I place everyone where I think they should be and let the accounting happen, I've done my part. I can't control what the others judges do. Skaters would do well to remember that—they can't control the judges, either."

When asked about skaters and parents who get nervous about judges, Rick comments, "I encourage parents to tell their children to focus on themselves. Don't focus on other competitors but try to outskate yourself. It helps in competition to focus on one element at a time. If you're thinking about competitors or the judges, you can't do your best. When you *do* see your marks, say, 4.5 for technical and a 5.0 for presentation, ask yourself what these marks are saying to you."

Rick has this to say about presentation in a competition: "Skaters should focus on their skating moves between jumps. I don't notice the costume as much as skaters and parents may think I do. A dress or smiling won't 'throw' a competition. I do look for the connection of the costume to the music. Overdone costumes may distract me. Only when someone is pushing the limits of the outfit do I react, like too brief or no skirt when that is the rule. I am not a drama expert, so I may not get what a costume is trying to convey. Overall, I've never seen a competition won or lost on an outfit."

Rick is open to the critique process. "It's common for us judges to do critiques before the qualifying competition to help evaluate how the skaters are doing. Coaches are looking for input and we give it. Different judges notice different things. The closer to a competition a critique occurs, of course, the less we'll say about making changes."

Rick adds this final bit of wisdom: "We expect skaters to be prepared, clean, and know what they're doing. As judges, we must also be prepared and know what we're doing, like the new rules for every year. Our sport has really taken off. We must, as judges, keep the integrity in it."

Charlie Cyr

Charlie Cyr has lived in the United States and Canada and has dual citizenship. His family lived in northern Maine in the town of Madawaska, across the river from Edmundston, New Brunswick. Charlie skated in Edmundston and trained in the summers in Moncton, Fredericton, and Saint John.

"I started skating late, at age sixteen, after playing ice hockey. Skiing was also important to me; I raced CAN-AM, and I was invited to try out for the Canadian National Ski Team. I played tennis as well. Later in my life, I acquired two black belts, one in Tang Soo Do and in American Shorin Ryu. I considered skating a hobby and a passion, but not my whole life. I skated singles, pairs, and dance, attaining a high level of expertise."

Education was also important to him. Charlie attended the University of Maine on a full scholarship, earned a bachelor's degree in research biology, and applied to medical school. When he did not get accepted, he enrolled in X-Ray technology training. He currently is the practice administrator of the Desert Orthopedic Center in Palm Desert,

California, managing eighty-five employees and the orthopedic practices of sixteen physicians. He is married and the father of two daughters.

Charlie first became a judge in Canada, advancing to National Canadian judge level in dance, singles, and pairs. When he moved to California in 1980, he had to serve as a trial judge at U.S. Nationals. "It took three years before my judging credentials were transferred to the United States," he notes.

From that point he was credentialed to be a U.S. National dance judge. Charlie recalls that another seven years were spent in obtaining his National pairs and singles judging credentials. He received an international dance appointment in 1993 and his international pairs and singles appointment in 1994. He served as team leader for several international competitions and two World Championships from 1994 to 1998, and most recently judged dance at the Championship Series Final in Munich. Charlie comments that he is eligible for his World and Olympic appointment. He also served at the USOC Training Center during the summer of 1998.

Charlie lives the principles he applies to his life both at work and as a skating judge. His life has been profoundly affected, he says, by the struggle his wife faced with the disease of alcoholism. Charlie was primary parent for his two girls for eight months while his wife was in a full-time treatment program. "I did a lot of growing at that time," he reports. "I realized there was life beyond skating and judging. Our family learned not to take things for granted." He talks of the positive influence on his life of the Twelve Step Program, a series of commitments and activities that help (him) keep things in perspective.

Now, with his wife active in her recovery, Charlie can more freely devote time to judging. "Hard work and my persistence has paid off in judging," he says. "My performing as a skater also has helped me in my job. I travel all over the world now and have become more tolerant of people who aren't like me."

What does Charlie advise skaters about putting judging in perspective for themselves?

"Judges are going to be there, judging at a competition, whether you want them to be or not. So, why worry about them? Think about what you want to do in your skating. Imagine, if there were no medals given in a competition, what would you want to say to yourself about your performance?"

Charlie also remarks about the impatience he sees in skaters, a phenomenon that troubles him. "I see skaters beginning at step one of something but wanting step fifteen right away, with little acceptance of the reality of the progression to get there. Those kinds of expectations lead to their feeling pressured. No bad days can be allowed. When you are so impatient to 'get there,' it's harder to learn from your mistakes or to turn around a difficult time. This life seems so fast-paced. But skating takes time, just like learning to walk took time. How much time are you willing to put into skating to learn it well? When you do have a bad day, do you come out of it smiling and smarter?

"I also see that some skaters want to hear only praise instead of honesty and constructive criticism from their coaches. I notice that if the coach says something that isn't positive, the skater may take it as 'the coach doesn't like me,' instead of using it to improve." He would encourage such skaters to look at criticism and mistakes in a new way, as information for growth.

From his own skating experience, Charlie tells this story. "I failed my fifth test eight times. I passed my first, second, third, and fourth tests the first time I tried. People would wonder how I kept on. It seemed to me that I was beginning to try too hard and had become obsessed with advancing in the sport. I lost the balance I'd had before. I had become my own worst enemy, my test judges told me. So, I started working on my sixth test, and then had new goals. I came back to my fifth test and passed it.

"My advice to skaters is to set goals and have a good time as well. It is great to want to excel in skating. It's also important to ask yourself, 'what will I do with my life after this sport?'"

When asked about what he looks for as a judge, Charlie is candid. "I think of the total package, the total person. I'll remember the skater who is nice off the ice. I think of Tonia Kwaikowski, who didn't make it to the Olympics or qualify to go to Worlds, but finally went as an alternate and came in sixth. She was so gracious. I think of Michelle Kwan, and her graciousness when she won Olympic silver. I felt for her. She is a nice person off the ice. I also felt for Lu Chen at the Nagano Olympics. Here are three shining examples of women who will go far, long after they are no longer skating. There is only one gold medal at a competition so it's important to feel a part of something when you compete and to feel satisfied with what you have."

Jon Jackson

"I began skating at the age of twelve, which is considered late in the sport of figure skating. I understood from the beginning that age was against me. However, I excelled rapidly, and was competing as a Novice by age sixteen, and as a Junior by age seventeen, having twice qualified for the Sectional championships.

"As a competitor, I did not handle the pressure well. I skated fine in practice, but poorly in competition. My anxiety was due, in part, to the fact that I didn't understand the system of judging. Skaters won medals, I mistakenly thought, because the judges 'liked' them.

"By the time I was skating at the Junior level in my final year of high school, I realized that the time commitment required to excel in skating at a competitive level would conflict with my desire to attend college. I chose to attend college, a decision I have never regretted.

"At the University of Utah, my undergraduate major was finance. After earning my bachelor's degree, I took a year off to work, then pursued a master's in business, then attended and completed law school. I am now a practicing attorney in San Francisco, focusing on analysis, planning, and advising for corporate clients in California and Oregon.

"My clients and associates have been quite understanding about my judging, which is a tremendously time-intensive volunteer activity. I got my start in judging while I was still in high school, working part time at the rink. There was an opportunity to do a little trial judging when I was sixteen and seventeen, and my curiosity about it led me to participate in the events that were available to me at that age. Later, I served on the board of directors for the Utah Figure Skating Club, so I still felt involved in skating, even though I had stopped competing.

"World Judge Ida Tateoka approached me, suggesting I seriously pursue judging. The accelerated program had just been started in 1983 by the USFSA, so I signed on and completed a year of trial judging, receiving my low test appointment in 1984. From that point onward, my appointments came quickly. For a time, I judged ice dancing as well as singles and pairs.

"Ida Tateoka and many other committed volunteers in the sport were early influences on my judging development. From them, I learned that you must be very committed to judging because it takes so much time to develop an awareness of the rules, sensibilities, and judgment that contribute to being a good judge.

"In 1993, I was appointed a national judge and was officially listed as an international judge by the ISU in 1996. Each major competition generally requires the investment of a week of my time. I have a strong desire to attend every event to which I am invited. I find a way to attend as many as I can fit into my schedule.

"Most recently, in addition to local judging, I judged at Skate America in the fall of 1996 in Massachusetts; at a Junior competition in Slovenia in the spring of 1997; at a Junior competition in St. Gervais, France, in the fall of 1997; and at the Junior Series Final in March, 1998, in Lausanne, Switzerland.

"I enjoy seeing the caliber of skating that is presented at high-level competitions. I also appreciate the friendships I've developed with other judges, coaches, and skaters. The most valued aspect of attending any competition is the opportunity to spend time with them. Participating in the sport gives me a sense of self-satisfaction in that I can extend myself to others who appreciate and value my time, expertise, and friendship.

"The greatest challenge in judging, in my opinion, is to be fair. The only way to be completely fair is to have a thorough understanding of the rules. Ironically, you must also accept that you never know everything, and will necessarily continue to learn over time, whether from another judge, a coach, or from your own mistakes.

"I don't worry too much whether I agreed with my peers on the panel. I am more concerned that I do what I think is fair. Sometimes it is clear; other times it is not. With experience, judging does get easier but is no less challenging. Every challenge is accompanied by anxiety. I can empathize with the skaters, not only as a former skater having experienced the same anxiety they are feeling, but also as a judge. The anxiety that accompanies this uncertainty is imposing, but developing the perspective and credentials necessary to perform well requires repeated exposure to uncertainty."

"What can I advise a skater who is nervous about competition? I would remind skaters that they *do have control* over specific things that are being judged. In judging technical merit, the ISU (with the USFSA exactly following their lead) instructs judges to take into consideration four factors: the difficulty, variety, cleanness/sureness, and speed of a performance. In judging for presentation, judges must take into consideration seven factors in singles skating: variation of speed; utilization of the ice surface; easy movement and sureness in time to the music; carriage and style; originality; and expression of the character of the music; with an eighth factor considered for pairs, unison of movement.

"These specifics are in the rule books issued by the ISU and the USFSA. There *is* something quantifiable about each of these factors. The skater *can* have control over his or her marks if mindful of these elements during their training. A skater should do his or her best to excel in these *very specific, quantifiable* factors. This means that, in training, a skater might work on moves in the field to improve the carriage and style element of their presentation mark, or work on the skating edge into and out of a jump to improve the technical merit mark. If the work is done during the training season, the skater will have more control over their markings and ultimate placement, which, in turn, should lessen their anxiety.

"It's a myth that judges decide 'how we feel' about a skater in making the marks. Rather, the seven elements that make up the presentation mark and the four elements of the technical merit mark control the judging. If skaters would seize upon these concepts as listed in the rule book, they would quickly rise above the rest, if only because so few do. How skaters skate in competition is a direct result of how they train. If a skater is properly trained, having focused on these factors in practice, he or she will have control over everything that the judge is looking for.

"What happens when judges come to practice at a competition? While what I see in practice is related to what I might see in competition, I judge solely the performance presented in the competition itself. Watching a skater practice gives me a foundation for judging the event: a sense of the level of difficulty of the program, the variety of technical elements, utilization of the ice surface, those things that, in all likelihood, will not change from practice to competition. From this I gain a base understanding so that I don't begin at ground zero when I see the performance. I have twenty seconds to make a mark during competition. For the mark to accurately reflect the skating performed, I must have that base to begin from. The result is that the marks reflect the way the skater skates at the time that it counts—in the competition itself.

"What about a situation when judges disagree? Disagreement amongst the judges is terribly misunderstood. Obviously, when it happens, the parents and skaters ask why. And they generally ask the coach. The coaches do their best to answer the parent and skater. This explanation may itself contribute to the misunderstanding. Rather than asking why, or proffering an explanation, the skaters and coaches should appreciate that different perspectives are brought to the sport, and that a majority of the panel determines the winner. How unfair our system of judging would be if the judges were always in agreement (and how corrupt it sometimes looks when this is the case).

"The skaters, coaches, and parents should always feel free to discuss the judging with the officials. When asked to justify my marks, I find my 'grounding' in the rules. I go back to the concepts outlined in the rule book. In this way, I can offer quantifiable reasons that may better help the skater understand the placement and improve a future performance.

"Sometimes placements differ because there are so many quantifiable elements to consider. One judge may have overlooked one particular element, while others may have overemphasized it. There is so much to look at and evaluate in so little time. Even beyond the basic four elements for technical merit and the seven elements for presentation, are sub-elements. Evaluating the difficulty of the program, for example, requires the consideration of many things: the jumps, spins, the footwork, the movements, the entry into elements, and so on. Sometimes the differences in these elements and sub-elements is minute between two, three, or even more skaters, which results in disparate results. But this is no more a criticism of the judging than it is a criticism of the skating. The differences in the judges' marks can be appreciated when skaters and coaches respect the competency of the judging panel and understand quantifiable aspects of judging.

"For me to be fair, I have to be quantitative. I wish I had done that as a skater, and focused on the quantifiables. I would have been a lot less nervous. When I am asked for advice, I tell skaters and coaches that the main emphasis is training. Training is a disciplined series of habits—habits that incorporate the elements outlined in the rule book. Skating is a *sport.*"

Part Five

Special Topics

Chapter Thirteen
Pair Skating

Tracy: I can relate to the excitement people feel when they watch an elite pair team, because my brother Scott and I skated pairs together from the time I was eight and he was ten. Competing nationally and internationally was really exciting for me.

In this chapter, I tell you what I do when training young pair teams. I then offer tips for executing the tricks of pair skating without trying to provide specific instruction, which is impossible in just one chapter. I talk about finding an appropriate partner and comment on the logistical challenges. Then my brother Scott shares his insider tips on skating pairs from the man's perspective.

TRAINING YOUNG PAIR TEAMS

One of the things you'll notice about a young boy and girl in their first pair lesson is that they may be shy and uncomfortable holding hands with each other. This connection is the first they must make to become a successful team, however, so I approach this subject in a businesslike manner, being well aware that they probably wouldn't be holding hands at school, either.

I have them stand side by side and look into a mirror, and show them in a matter-of-fact way the correct positioning and alignment of their bodies when they are holding hands. I tell them that in pair skating each one is an extension of the other. I have them stand tall and practice matching positions with one another, encouraging them to strive for similar lines of the arms and angles of the head. Once they have mastered alignment while in the tall stance, I instruct them to do the same in a bent-knee position.

On the ice, I start them off with forward crossovers in a hand-to-hand position and teach them to skate in a clockwise and counterclockwise direction. Then I teach them to skate a little closer in the Kilian position. Finally, I teach them to skate backward in a clockwise and counterclockwise direction.

The young pair must learn what is called proper tracking, meaning that the boy stays right in line with his partner while skating forward on the same curve. I explain to the girl that she must stay right in line with her partner while skating backward on the same curve.

I stress the importance of their learning to match one another. They must develop the same rhythm, amount of lean and extension, and depth of their knee bend. When they get comfortable with skating crossovers, I begin teaching them side-by-side maneuvers, starting with one-foot spins. I demonstrate how they must watch each other as they enter into the spin to create the same lobe (arc of a circle) on the ice while skating side by side.

I talk with them about my belief that each pair team needs a leader and ask who is most comfortable in that role. I explain that pair skating must have one partner who calls out the counts and who takes responsibility for quick decisions. The leader is often the boy, but not always. Once the decision is made about the leader, I help them establish a definite game plan so each one knows what to do.

By watching other pair teams, they begin to understand the idea of synchronizing their movements and developing their skill in skating, quite literally, as the extension of the other. Certain qualities must emerge from their partnership for the pair to be successful. The leader must maintain the role of directing their skating and show how he or she can persevere under pressure. The partner who is designated as the follower must demonstrate a willingness in taking instructions from the leader. Each one must be comfortable in his or her role, with the leader offering consistent guidance and the follower trust and responsiveness. Once in a great while, I find a pair team that can trade roles and make it work but this is rare. It sometimes happens in elite pair teams who have skated together for many years.

PAIR TRICKS

Let me briefly describe the tricks in pairs that make this form of skating so exciting. The categories of tricks are lifts and twists, pair spins, side-by-side spins, side-by-side jumps, throw jumps, and death spirals.

Lifts/Twists
The lift is recognizable as the trick in which the man lifts the lady up, elevating her off the ice. There are many types of lifts, starting with the basic hand-to-body hold with its numerous variations. There are also hand-to-hand lifts that involve the lady changing position in the air and utilizing creative dismounts.

Beginning teams start with the man fully extending his right arm as he lifts while his left hand supports the lady at about the height of his shoulder. At the Intermediate level, you'll see a hand-to-hand press lift in which both of his arms are fully extended. At the Novice, Junior, and Senior levels, the man lifts the lady over his head with just one arm fully extended.

One-handed Table Top Lift—Luke and Laura Muana. ©David Madison 1998

Back Press Lift—Dave Delago and Whitney Gaynor. ©David Madison 1998

The tabletop (or platter) lift has a distinctive look because the man lifts the lady like a platter. The basic two-handed press lift is one of the first overhead lifts taught to pair teams. In the top photo on the previous page, Luke and Laura are executing a variation of the tabletop lift that has a high degree of difficulty because Luke is holding her with only one arm. This particular lift is executed by more advanced pair teams. In the bottom photo on the previous page, Dave and Whitney are doing a back hand-to-hand press lift, also called a hand-to-hand loop lift.

The man should have complete control of his footwork as he lifts the lady while moving and flowing across the ice. In training the man to do lifts, I work with him to develop the proper Mohawks that take him across the rink, moving along in a straight path.

The responsibility of the lady is to hold her body positions tight and still while in the air, with good extensions. The term for a lift on which she changes positions in the air is a combination lift. If she is thrown up in the air while in a split position, rotates while descending, and is caught by the man, it is called a split twist lift. There are also lifts named for their take-off positions, such as the loop lift, the flip lift, the Lutz lift, and the Axel lift.

Position from a combination pair spin—Dave Delago and Whitney Gaynor.
©David Madison 1998

Spins

In pair spins, the partners skate on identical lobes, meet at the center point, and grab hold of one another while each is spinning on one foot. Usually, the first spin partners learn is the pair camel and its several variations, in which one or both partners spins in the camel position.

In the photo at the top of the next page, Luke holds Laura by clasping his right hand to his left wrist around the small of her back. He assumes a sit position, and she stretches her free leg back and extends her arms in the pair sit position.

Pair Sit Spin—Luke and Laura Muana. ©David Madison 1998

Side By Side Sit Spins in unison— Whitney Gaynor and Dave Delago. ©David Madison 1998

In solo spins, the partners are spinning side by side in unison. The critical factor is to synchronize the movements so they enter and come out of the spin at exactly the same time, and complete the same number of rotations in unison.

Side-by-Side Jumps
In these tricks, the partners must execute their individual jumps in perfectly matched patterns, and the takeoffs, landings, air positions, and size of the jumps must be synchronized. When partners first learn these jumps, they generally keep some distance between them, although a team may be marked down if there is too much space. Elite pair teams jump much closer together, sometimes only fingertips apart. The rule books govern the types of side-by-side jumps required and their levels of difficulty.

Throw Jumps

This trick, in my opinion, is the coolest thing ever invented. For the lady, it feels like you're in flight. The man's assistance, or throw, gives the lady her momentum to fly. These are now required in the pair short program, as well as in the long. My former pair coach, Ron Ludington, invented the throw Axel as well as many of the other pairs elements performed today.

The woman's responsibility in the throw jumps is to feel her takeoff and react to the timing of the throw with her own jump action. You generally see throw Axels, Salchows, toe loops, and loops. They can be singles, doubles, or triples. We will probably see throw quads in the near future.

Death Spirals

This is a trick in which the man executes a pivot on his toe pick while turning the woman around him in a death spiral position. There are four types of death spirals: the forward inside, which is the most common; the back inside; the backward outside; and the forward outside, which is the least common. The three more common death spirals are required in both the short and long program.

The only contact point the man has with his partner is through his right hand. The fascinating part of this trick is that the lady's head should lower as close to the ice as possible without touching it. Her free hand can't touch the ice, either. Her position must be stable and solid, which requires years of training to get it right. The judges look closely at the man to see that he has completed at least one full revolution on his toe pick in the pivot position.

Backward Inside Death Spiral—Whitney Gaynor and Dave Delago. ©David Madison 1998

Back Outside Death Spiral—Luke and Laura Muana. ©David Madison 1998

MY EXPERIENCES

My experience as the female pair partner was like getting on the wild rides at an amusement park. Lifts can remind the lady what it's like to stop abruptly at the top of the Ferris wheel. The best pair teams learn to savor the ride and enjoy their tricks more than feel afraid. At times, I was really scared to be up in the air over Scott's head because I had a fear of heights. However, the more pair skating I did with Scott, the more I liked it and the more I got over my fear.

With Scott, I was skating with someone I respected. I loved to skate well with him in unison and to develop the capacity for skating together with good speed. To me, a pair team has the energy of two people united which is far greater than the energy of just one person on the ice. It was a feeling of power for me, of exceeding all my expectations. As we got better, we both acted like the leaders, and we could get competitive with one another. To me, Scott was the best skater in our rink, so he was my competition in a very real way. Did he get his triple toe? Then I better get mine, too.

By the time we reached Senior level and skated Nationals at Hartford in 1977, we had become well-rounded skaters and felt confident about what we could do. My mother had made sure that each of us had continued to skate singles, and that helped.

If Scott had picked another partner instead of skating with his sister, he probably would have picked someone with my skill level but who was no more than five feet tall. Scott was 5'6" and I was 5'3". When I talk to skaters about choosing a partner, I tell them about this reality. It's much easier to skate pairs if the man is six or more inches taller than the woman. Many pairs have men taller than the woman by a foot. In terms of weight, it is, of course, much easier for the man to lift a partner who weighs eighty pounds less than he does.

THOUGHTS ON CHOOSING A PARTNER AND LOGISTICS

If the prospective partners are close in height and weight, the man may face the prospect of compensating with intensive strength training, but sometimes it becomes a safety issue. He may simply not be tall enough or strong enough to put his prospective partner up in a lift in a way that is safe. I discourage skaters from choosing partners too close in size and weight primarily for safety reasons. The expectations for technical difficulty in pair programs are too great now. There are aesthetic issues as well, since judges and spectators seem to reward the teams who demonstrate control over their bodies and command of intricate tricks in pair skating.

When two prospective partners meet and try skating together, I ask them to give it a six-week trial and then reassess the possibility before committing to being a pair. The man must ascertain what strengths he needs in order to skate successfully with this particular partner. Meanwhile, I often encourage them to stay with their singles skating and to become familiar with ice dancing, if they don't do this already. Ice dance training can add much to pair skating.

I ask the prospective partners to consider their compatibility in appearance. Can this pair generate a look together? I think of several different looks. One is a classical

The look of a well-matched pair—Luke and Laura Muana. ©David Madison 1998

look, with clean elegant lines and a refined, almost timeless sense exemplified by many of the Russian teams. There is also an athletic look, with the man in particular appearing powerfully strong and quick. Kitty and Peter Carruthers, silver medalists in the 1984 Olympics, were very athletic. Kitty was fearless in their throw triples and lateral twists, and their size difference helped greatly. Canadians Isabelle Brasseur and Lloyd Eisler, who are both very athletic and creative, also work with a big size difference.

A third look is a contemporary one that features pop music and "chemistry" on the ice. Canadians Barbara Underhill and Paul Martini could really portray this modern look, although they had a wonderful range of styles from classical to athletic.

Let me turn now to the logistical issues that are crucial in deciding about forming a pair team. What are the ages and lifestyles of each partner? Who moves, if they live in different cities?

Most of the time, because there are so few male partners, the young woman will consider making the move. If she can't move, her family may offer to pay for the male partner to move near her. The woman's family should make clear, ideally in a written contract, what they are agreeing to provide for him when he arrives. This may just be moving expenses, or it can include nearly everything—room and board, ice time, lessons, ballet classes, physical therapy, the cost of the choreography, the music, and the costumes.

I encourage male partners to find work to help contribute to the considerable expense that pair skating involves and to provide for his own amenities. One advantage of skating pairs is that there is only one fee for pair lessons, choreography, and music editing.

To me, the real advantage of skating pairs is that you have another person there to share the same moments in skating, and that you are working together to create those wonderful moments. It can be lots of fun when your partner is someone who has a great personality, like my brother, who also has a very quick wit.

A partner's family can be a plus if they support you as a team. Two partners and their families respecting each other, and working to solve problems together, can be a very powerful force.

Ideally, both partners have the same degree of motivation and commitment to their training and to performing well. Differences in the level of commitment to time and effort can provoke conflict between partners and their families or whoever is paying the bills.

My advice to anyone considering a move to skate pairs is to take a look at the track record of the coach before you agree to train at his or her center. Look at the track record of the prospective partner. Ask questions about the family's support, emotionally and financially, for their child to skate pairs. Find out if your prospective partner's lifestyle is compatible with your own.

A MALE PERSPECTIVE ON PAIR SKATING

Scott: I think some accidents can occur in pair skating because of insufficient size and weight differences. A female partner who is only ten pounds lighter than her partner will be much more difficult for him to lift. For the man, that last lift is tough at the end of four and one-half minutes, even if the woman only weighs ninety pounds.

Likewise, if the female partner is nearly as tall as he is, the male partner will find himself with fewer seconds that the woman is in the air when they are executing twists. This means your execution has to be precise. If it isn't, accidents can happen.

When a woman is 5'0" and a man 6'2", the woman can be launched into the air at full speed. Thus, the element can go to its maximum. When the height difference is considerably less, there is not enough time for the woman to do the rotations in the air on a triple twist and still be caught safely. You'll likely see uneasiness or strain on the part of the man.

In pairs, the timing has to be so exact. You want every advantage you can have. To get your timing down, you must practice a lot. Even though we practiced for hours, I still couldn't rely solely on my timing, so we had to watch each other and adjust to one another as we skated. In our lifting practice off the ice, we had to remember that the timing was different on the ice and make the translation.

Because Tracy and I were so close in size, I appeared weak at times and had to work harder and get stronger. She was a great pair skater who loved to show off as a performer without ever being arrogant. However, when we skated around other pairs, it was really important for us never to look as if we were intimidated. "Show No Fear" was what our pair coaches taught us. This advice came in handy in elite competitions when other pairs skated close to you just to see if you'd look away. We didn't.

I remember some things that are good hints for those of you who skate pairs now. We learned our lifts in a swimming pool, which let us experiment and get it right with far less peril. It also really helps if the male partner doesn't look up at the woman when he is lifting her. It goes without saying that she shouldn't move her body excessively on a lift. She should hold strong positions and be as steady as possible in tricks like the tabletop lift. She should be sturdy. Fearlessness is a plus.

The man should work on skating good-quality Mohawks with shallow edges and smooth, rhythmic, and quiet turns. He and his partner should develop good close foot-work. Also, become adept at watching your partner. Practice imitating your partner enough so that you achieve the unison so valued in pair skating.

In pair sit spins, Tracy spun on her right foot. I'd lean back on the ball of my foot in a sit position and pull her into my spin to create the necessary rotational force. If your spins are slow (I say by way of a hint), don't put them at the end of the program.

It helped us to get the correct lift positions by practicing on the floor, which we did for an hour every day. We worked on our lifts repeatedly. We practiced in front of the mirror and then got on the ice and made the adjustments for the timing.

Tracy would do thousands of abdominal crunches to help her hold her positions in the air. In our twist lifts, the height similarity was really a problem. In this trick, the man must lift and throw simultaneously. In the twist lift, the woman must push off the man's wrists and go up well beyond his fully extended arms. In other words, she must be completely over his head. A man who is really strong can save a botched twist, catching her and putting her down. No matter what his size, it helps if the woman has incredible control over her body.

In a hint for dismounts, the man should bring the woman to the ice by bending his knees to decrease the distance that she must come down on her own. The idea is to set her down gently and softly.

The man sets the pattern into a lift. The woman's responsibility is to track him and stay in synch as he sets it up. On a throw jump, it's the man's responsibility not to throw the woman into the boards. Size differential is not as much of a problem in throw jumps, especially if the woman is a good jumper.

In death spirals, the man must bend back and remain still with his toe pick in the ice. I remember my heel used to be almost stabbing me in the rear end. The man trains his pivot by doing it repetitively, and he must learn to keep his right arm stiff.

I also want to say something about the advantages of being as close in size as we were. Our spins and side-by-side jumps were easier for us to coordinate than for other pairs. We got into unison much more easily, and we could quickly adapt and match body line, our positions, and lean angles.

When Tracy was injured and we had to stop our pair skating, I was approached by others who wanted to skate with me. Honestly, it would have felt strange to do the lifts and spins with someone else. Going on without Tracy wouldn't have meant much, so it was an easy decision for me to make. One month I was competing at Nationals, then she got hurt. By the next month, I was working and not skating.

In the end, she was out of skating and it was time for me to stop. We had reached the top of our game, and she helped me get there. It was a great ride.

Chapter Fourteen
Advice for Parents of Skaters

Tracy: I have been a coach for nine years and have come to appreciate the role that parents play in the well-being of the students I teach. Skaters' parents and extended family are their primary support group, the ones who are cheering, encouraging, and being enthusiastic about skating. As I see it, parents are also the most important influences in helping skaters develop what is so important, a balanced healthy life that has skating in it, and plans for life after skating.

Let me say first that I have great respect for the parents of my students and for parents all over the country who make the time and investment for their children to skate. May I also say that I see parenting as the hardest job there is; it is difficult to guide the development of a young person as he or she both participates in a demanding sport and participates in life. Because of this respect I hold for parents, I've thought carefully about the ideas that follow.

I think the best skating parent is one who allows the coach to coach, the judges to judge, and the officials to do their jobs—and, of course, who lets the skater be the one doing the skating. I think a skater is truly blessed whose parent sees his or her role as one of emotional nurturer. Such parents take care of needs from transporation to mailing applications on time, and are positive reinforcers, especially when a skater is feeling disappointed or discouraged. I value a parent who gets genuinely excited about the skater's accomplishments and progress but doesn't push. I also value the parent who can hear the coach's input when forming expectations for a skater's development and provide the resources to get there without trying to live vicariously through the child or insisting on the Olympics (or else).

When I think of a parent taking care of a skater's needs, I think of getting the child to the rink on time, every time, if at all possible. This extends to providing rides to conditioning classes, ballet, and to the competitions themselves. I also think it prevents undue pressure on the skater when a parent pays the lesson fees and other costs on time so the child doesn't have to relay requests from the coach or feel badly when bills are overdue. A helpful parent is one who keeps discussions about money for skating as a parental concern rather than the skater's worry. In my years in the skating world, I have witnessed the impact on a young person whose parent is more concerned with a return on the investment (that is, winning) than with the well-being of the child. Fortunately, this is rare, but the results can be damaging for a long time.

It asks a lot of a parent to approach competitions with a sense of fun and an attitude of wanting the child to skate his or her personal best, the theme of this book. This attitude of skating your best while focusing on what you can control helps a skater be less nervous about competing. It may seem a little strange, but the focus on performing one's best rather than on winning in a competition allows a skater to perform well before the judges. You, the parent, can support this attitude of personal best. This means that you, too, have to resist being caught up in worrying about things over which you have little control, such as what the judges decide and how the other competitors perform.

Competitions can be opportunities for skaters to grow in healthy ways if you can enjoy yourself while there and put your attention on making sure that needs are met: for the music to be handed to the official in charge, for your skater to be rested and well nourished, for making sure the costume, makeup, if used, and hair are just right, and maneuvering the camera, of course!

Competitions can be remembered by skaters as disasters or opportunities. How *you* respond has a crucial impact here. For your skater to learn to win graciously and to keep disappointments in perspective, your reassurance that he or she is still loved, valued, and cared for, whatever the posted results, is key.

This is no small challenge. I know it's hard to watch your child fall during a program. You can be horrified. Alternatively, you can think about the lessons learned, and your child's choice to get up quickly, while smiling, continuing on, and leaving behind what just happened. Your own perspective about this sport will help at those moments, when drying your child's tears and helping him or her cope with what feels right then like total embarrassment. Skaters fall during practice and fall during a competition. Going for everything a skater has been working on can be a motivating, fear-dissolving attitude to bring to a short program. Striving out there, and skating your best—rather than holding back for fear of looking foolish—these are other perspectives you can encourage after a skate that your child finds disappointing.

What if your child is really upset by a competition and doesn't want to compete again? First, listen well and hear your child's feelings. Then try to evaluate the situation objectively with your child and the coach. As clearly as possible, go back over what happened. What were the difficulties? What could be taken from this situation and applied to creating a better experience for your child in the future, not just to achieve a winning performance. My hope is that you will build a support system for skating, including the competition process, and form a united front that reduces friction among the members of your team so your skater can do his or her personal best.

When it's the parent who is nervous about the competition, I try to reassure that parent. I know I don't want to shift my focus from the child to taking care of the parent, but fathers and mothers do get anxious. I prefer that the parent who is worrying aloud be willing to hand the skater over to me and then keep a distance. Kids sense your nervousness. After consultation with the coach, it may be best for you to stay up in the stands, making your presence known to your child but keeping your worries more private. You can be helpful and available from this perch and yet not add to the stress your child may be feeling.

I like to suggest to parents before competitions that they practice in their own heads being relaxed and calm at the competition site, that they imagine themselves being supportive and taking things in stride, that they feel themselves able to enjoy being there and roll with whatever the results are, and that they hear themselves saying to their skaters how proud they are of the progress being demonstrated on the ice.

With practice, these imagined states of mind can become your actual behavior at a competition. To me, this is one way you can be a personal best parent. The better you are as a skating parent, the more you help your skater skate his or her personal best.

What if your child truly skated his or her personal best and came in last? What should a parent do? I might first say what *not* to do. I hope you would not tell your child that his skating days are over. I would hope that you would not go into a tirade about the bad judging or some unfair advantage you think the competitors had over your child. I hope you would not fire the coach on the spot.

Instead, my advice is to take some time, maybe away from the competition site, and meet with the coach to make a realistic appraisal of the situation. If the child has just moved into the next higher level, this low placement may reflect that recent change. The skater may have reached a level where his natural talent and time to train are exceeded by what his competitors are able to do. It also helps to remember that, at Junior and Senior level in a National competition, there may be little detectable difference in the skating between the person placing first and the person in the last position because everyone is so good.

What if your child didn't seem to try during that short program? Before you express your dismay or anger, think about questions you might ask, like "What was happening for you out there? What were the distractions or other things getting in the way?" Please wait for your child's answers; don't jump in with your own interpretations. Your facial expression and how your voice sounds make a difference as you ask these questions. Being patient and concerned without overwhelming your child may help him or her open up to you. It's possible that your child truly doesn't want to compete. You need to let that be OK, regardless of your fantasies about the Olympics, agents, and endorsements.

Before a competition you must face all those hours of waiting. During this time, what does your child need from you specifically? Find out. Allow your child what he or she needs, within reason. If your child wants you to be close by, please do that. If your child likes lots of pumping up, please get into it. Sometimes a child would prefer to be with friends instead of you. If so, let that be all right with you and graciously say, "Have a good time."

If you don't know what to do or what to say, sort that out with your child's coach. If you know (or your child tells you) that you make your child nervous, definitely talk to the coach. In this case, handing your child over to the coach can take the pressure off you and your skater. Just make it your business to see what is needed to help your skater have the most positive competition experience possible.

Over the years, I've seen a variety of responses to competing. Some skaters love to perform, and really get into feeling, "Watch me, look at me." Others work hard to prepare, but they don't seem to have this same desire to be noticed yet want encouragement from their families. Still others are unsure about competing, or have to get used to it. Listen to your child. Let the child's preferences inform you. No matter how your child takes to competing, she needs you to stand behind her. She needs your response to be one of support and of taking the whole competition thing in stride.

I've noticed that when skaters start competing at a young age, they *do* seem to take it in stride. Attending your child's ballet recitals, concerts, and soccer games early on also helps the child feel comfortable about demonstrating things that have been learned and practiced.

It's a good idea for you, the parent, to discuss with the coach what competitions the child should enter during the skating season. Ultimately, it is best to leave the final say up to the coach about whether the skater is ready to enter any particular competition that was discussed earlier. A skater at lower levels needs a minimum of six weeks of preparation beforehand; without that, it is likely that the experience won't be favorable. As Sam and I discuss elsewhere in this book, preparation is one great way to reduce nervousness about competing.

At times parents have asked me what advice I have when a skater is being teased by other skaters at the rink. I try to find out if it's good-natured and friendly teasing, which commonly happens. Skaters spend a lot of time with each other and get on one another's nerves.

The teasing may follow a skater's winning result at a competition and be prompted by jealousy, especially if the child's win was unexpected by others. I might have the parent think about what the child has been acting like since the win. Has he or she been behaving in an arrogant way? Has he or she been acting differently and perhaps not being kind to the others?

If the teasing follows a difficult competition for the child, has he or she then been upset and difficult to be around, or a poor loser? If the parent tells me that the teasing seems out of line and very hurtful, I may step in and talk to the other skaters myself. I do this rarely, and only when it feels like I really should intervene. Otherwise, I ask the parent to have a serious talk with the child about what triggered the teasing. It may be best for the skater to use this unpleasant interaction as a motivator to train harder. A child learning how to persist, even with this adversity, will gain something about handling difficulties later in life. I talk to a skater and ask him or her to take a long look inside. I ask, "How do you respond when you win? How do you cope when you are disappointed? If you get upset, what does your behavior look like to those around you?"

When I was skating, I found it worked well for me to behave in a kind way to other skaters and to be respectful of coaches, other skaters' parents, and the judges and officials for their roles and responsibilities. On the other hand, I found it was important, even as a child, to learn to be assertive on the ice, to show that I was serious about my skating without being aggressive or rude. When I received good marks from judges, I felt glad but did not brag or look down on my competitors. I remembered that I did not completely control those marks, the judges did. I reminded myself to keep my perspective about what I could control—my efforts in practice and bringing my best to the competition. The judges might decide on a different outcome at the next competition. That's the great leveler in skating, and why it helps to concentrate on your skating and what you can do yourself.

One situation that comes up occasionally that demands a lot of a coach and the parent in how to handle it is when a skater seems to have difficulty moving beyond a certain point. Your child is toppling over while trying to master a flying spin and becomes frustrated. Or he is struggling to land a jump and it just isn't working. (The double Axel comes to mind.) The coach becomes concerned about the lack of progress and has the child work in the harness on the jump, but then the child balks when attempting the element out of the harness. You see tears, distress, and then hear, "I can't do it. I don't know if I want to skate anymore." Or the young man gets moody and comes late to lessons. What can a parent do to be supportive when a skater seems stuck?

Depending on your child's age and temperament, you may first want to discuss what's happening with the coach without your child present. I really urge you to be straightforward in expressing what you observe and how your child is talking about skating when he's away from the rink. The coach may not be as aware of the upset or frustration as you are. Tell him or her what your child's emotional response really is.

Several factors could explain your child's difficulty. You might already have a hunch. If so, offer it. Otherwise, I encourage you to consider the possibility that your child's physical development may lag behind the demands of the element that is so troubling. There are several physical factors that can delay a skater's progress in landing an Axel or executing a difficult spin.

Has your child had a growth spurt recently? This can affect balance and coordination. Your child's upper-body strength may be less developed than is necessary to rotate rapidly and check out quickly. A skater may not have a good sense of where his body is in space, and this may become more obvious as the level of difficulty increases for jumps and spins. In talking the situation over with the coach, keep in mind that additional information may be helpful, such as the expert opinion of your child's sports medicine physician, the conditioning instructor or athletic trainer, a podiatrist (foot specialist), or a physical therapist experienced in evaluating figure skaters. You may hear from one or more of these experts that your child would benefit from orthotics, additional conditioning training, or simply more time to grow. Please seek out and use this information before you decide to take your child out of skating.

There is also the more common situation where a younger skater has been winning competitions but then no longer does so well at the Juvenile level or above because of poorer technical marks. What may be occurring here is that this skater has reached the point where the more technically skilled skaters have surpassed him or her. This can be incredibly frustrating for you and of course, for your child.

What do I recommend? I talk to the parent and child about focusing on artistic programs or trying out ice dancing or precision skating. Or that they give some thought to skating exhibitions and moving away from the competitive scene altogether. I make these suggestions with great care and regard for the skater's feelings when it has been my responsibility to set up this talk. I do not want a child to get the impression that these ideas are the booby prize for not landing her double Axel or Salchow. These are ideas that may lead the skater to a better fit, to finding the right niche for this phase of his or her skating involvement.

Once in a while, if it seems appropriate, I will share my own story of being kicked out of ballet class by the teacher when I was only six. Yes, it's true that I dreamed of being a great dancer. It's also true that, back then, I lacked body awareness and couldn't hold the basic positions. My muscles seemed loose, and I was spindly and didn't have the balance and coordination of the other girls in the class. My mother told me she thought it was fine that I leave the class, and she did her best to explain to me that I wasn't physically strong enough to do what was required. She also reminded me how many times I'd come home from class crying about not being able to what the other girls did so easily.

Yes, I was devastated. But today, I am so glad she could see that my leaving the class was the best thing. Otherwise, I wouldn't have turned to skating, which my physical development at that time allowed me to progress in much more easily. I took to singles skating quickly, had no fear, and seemed to be able to do just about anything my coach asked me to do.

Eventually, I took ballet classes again. I had trained enough on and off the ice that my balance and coordination allowed me to be OK in a dance class and later to excel. Finally, as a professional skater, I was cast in a production with skaters who had all been former ballerinas except for me.

Looking back, I wish that, when I was six, the ballet teacher could have told me to leave in a much more supportive way. This is why I ask you as a parent to handle this situation carefully and hope that coaches will, as well. Now I think the teacher really did me a favor after all. I had the opportunity to find the right thing for me.

Children have different capabilities. Your challenge as a parent, and mine as a coach, is to guide that young person in finding the best fit so that personal best is possible.

PARENTS SHARE THEIR EXPERIENCES

To give added perspective to this chapter on advice of parents of skaters, Sam and I asked three skating parents—Dierdre Fujimoto, Karen Verili, and Gail Erb—to share their experiences in this chapter. Deirdre Fujimoto is the mother of two of my students, Jena and Cali. Deirdre is a parent who really supports her two girls and is a resource for the skating club and the other parents in it. Gail Erb is the mother of my student, Rebecca Erb, who has competed nationally and internationally in pairs and skated in the 1998 National Championships as a Novice Lady. Karen Verili is the mother of Jennifer Verili, a former national competitor in singles. Karen has been involved with the USFSA Parents' Committee since its founding in 1992.

Deirdre Fujimoto, Skating Parent
"I was an only child and my parents did a lot for me. I was a swimmer and my mother would drive me to practice and on weekends, she'd take me a hundred miles to the meets.

"My wanting to do a lot for my girls comes directly from my own experience growing up.

"Jena said early on that she wanted to try skating, at age four. We found a rink only ten mintues away, and she started with group lessons twice a week. We found a coach, Tracy, and followed her to another rink a much greater distance from home. It's five days a week now, early mornings, in rush hour traffic.

"The girls are home-schooled, but not just because of skating. Jena was a serious student in private school but also felt bored and that she didn't have much time, with skating and ballet. The home schooling also lets us take vacations in a more flexible way, especially since my husband, who's an oral surgeon, finds it difficult to get away.

"Skating is a subjective sport. I was in an objective sport—swimming. In a swim match, it's who gets there the fastest that wins. The subjectivity of skating is sometimes frustrating for Jena. She was a hot shot at ages six and seven, then others started to pass her by in the competition results.

"I told her then and tell her now that she can't completely control the judging. I tell her, 'Skate for yourself,' because that's what makes sense to me in this sport.

"I also tell her, 'Do your best,' and 'You have a life outside of skating.' I want her to keep the perspective about skating. She was having trouble with that perspective when she was trying to get her Axel. She wanted to get it badly—but she wanted it for us and for Tracy, even though none of us pressured her. Then she got injured and was off the ice for a long time. I knew, but then she started to realize, that it was OK if she didn't skate. Her whole outlook then changed.

"Jena came back to skating after her injury. This time she stopped trying so hard. Her Axel came and then she starting getting her doubles. It was a learning experience for me, how Jena and other skaters I've seen can get so caught up in doing things like the others are doing. It can lead to wanting more lesson time, feeling upset, or questioning. I know for me it is sometimes hard to figure out what is showing interest in your child's skating and what is pushing too hard.

"I try not to watch too often at lessons because I can get upset if I feel like Jena or Cali is not trying, and I don't want to feel bad like that. So, I do work in my car or I walk; I know now it's best for me not to watch all the time, like some parents do. I let the girls know I want them to use the lesson time well, and I want them to know that skating should be fun for them, too. We also have routines now where they must play their program music at least once during the public session, outside of their lesson.

"I don't feel comfortable demanding that every second of lesson time be used well. There are parents who expect that, because skating takes so much time and costs so much money. I don't think kids should do that. I also think it's good to leave the skating at the rink and go on to other things. Jena has friends in ballet, which she goes to three times a week. She has a special friend outside of skating, one she knows from her days being at school. Cali makes friends everywhere.

"I don't think of myself as an expert on the skating stuff. But I do think that parents' expectations can be higher than is realistic, like when they ask the coach, 'Why can't she do this?' without giving it a chance. I see that children learn at different rates. I've ob-served in the seven years I've been around that every skater has trouble with some element. It also has been my observation that if a skater can stick to what he or she is trying to learn, and the parent can be patient, that it will probably come."

Karen Verili, Skating Parent

"Before I say anything else, I am first a parent to two grown daughters, Lisa and Jennifer, of whom I am very proud. Jennifer is now twenty-four and lives in Salt Lake City. She still loves to skate and is building a career as a skating coach.

"Jennifer started skating at age eight. She was very gutsy and loved the challenge of jumping, mastering all her triple jumps except for the triple Axel. Her accomplishments include being a three-time Junior Ladies and two-time Senior Ladies Regional Freeskating Champion, Senior Ladies Sectional Champion, and three-time national competitor. The biggest accomplishment, in my opinion, is being able to look back and see that she maintained through the bad times as well as the good. She finished what she set out to do—to compete and perform well at every level of the sport through many years of hard work.

"The journey from the wobbly-legged little girl hanging on the rail to the top level of a sport as highly competitive as figure skating is a very difficult one. I can best describe it as an E-ticket ride at Disneyland: you wait in line forever, people think you are a little crazy, you finally get on and you think you're crazy, the ride is a thrill a minute and you think you are going to lose it; but when it's over and you get off, you are really glad you did it. And if you had the time and money, you'd get right back on and do it again!

"As a parent, any goals for Jennifer were really quite simple—be the best that you can be and have a good time in the process—which is easier said than done. It was important to her father and me that Jennifer would remember her skating career as a positive part of her development. Her continued love of the sport and involvement in the skating environment today, both professionally and personally, attests to the fact that skating has been a positive force in her life, and for that I am grateful. This has made all the sacrifices worthwhile.

"Being so involved in skating, I know that the better a child does, the more money it costs. This is the reality that must be taken seriously by parents. However, they must not expect that what they spend will ever result in a financial return or future payoff. That's too much pressure on a child. The money should be spent with the intention that it allows your child to develop as far as he or she can. It is your contribution, and you have the control to spend or not to spend. It's not your child's fault that you have spent so much. It's your decision and you own it, and so you must live with it.

"From being around this sport so long, I know that parents can nurture their children in skating just like anything else kids do. But you can't make someone a champion and you can't buy a champion. It seems that some parents have the idea that if they provide the best coaching, equipment, and costumes, the result should be a winner. As a skater takes the final step to the top, the field narrows. All have talent or they wouldn't be there. At that point, it's the special combination of person, discipline, being free of injury, the right timing, and some luck. Much of the time it requires living and training away from home. Not every child or parent can do that comfortably.

"My time as a skating parent when Jennifer was younger meant getting up at 4:00 A.M. and driving to the rink. I will always cherish the memories of this time spent with my good friend and mentor, Carole Yamaguchi. We would park next to each other in the parking lot of the rink in the exact same spot every day, every year, making sure that Jennifer and Kristi got inside OK. I got my best sleep in my car; and when I wasn't sleeping, I was beading costumes.

"Carole and I would go inside when the freestyle session began. I expected Jennifer to be on the ice, on time. I felt it was good to have that consistency of my being there. Kids will be kids, and I wanted her to be disciplined about time and to develop good work habits. I expected her to use her training time well.

"I liked to watch her lessons. I loved to watch her out there trying, seeing the joy on her face when she accomplished something she was working on. I wouldn't have wanted to miss that.

"I worked full time while she skated although I left a corporate position to take a job in a professional office, where I still am now. I did so because it allowed me the flexible hours I needed for getting Jennifer from place to place and for traveling to competitions. Carole Yamaguchi also came to work in this same office, that of a doctor whose son was also a national competitor. It definitely was a skating office! Carole and I are still very close friends, as are Kristi and Jennifer. As a skating parent, Carole is the ultimate role model. I have learned so much from her example: never put your child the skater above your child the child, and never allow yourself to lose your integrity as a parent.

"Skating took on a life of its own for me, as well as for Jennifer. In addition to my full time job, I started making costumes, first for Jennifer, then for local, national, and international skaters. My involvement with the USFSA also escalated. I believe that if you want to be proactive, you should participate in some aspect of the sport. I became active in our local club, serving on the board of directors and volunteering my time at local competitions.

"Still thinking I didn't have enough to do, I became the chair of Skater Services when Skate America, Worlds, and the 1996 National Championships were held in our local area. Skater Services is located near 'kiss and cry' at major competitions and provides costume repair, hair styling, makeup, skate sharpening, and a hangout for skaters before they go on the ice. I thought of this service as the '911 of skating' during competitions.

"I have also been a USFSA Parents' Committee member since its inception. Carole Yamaguchi was the first chairperson. This committee writes a newsletter for parents and organizes the informational meetings at the regional, sectional, and national competitions. When hosting these meetings, I am asked numerous questions by parents of younger skaters, parents who are eager to make the right choices for their children. For example, when a new parent asks me about finding a coach, I suggest that he or she observe a prospective coach working with other students during lessons and at competitions to see how that coach handles stressful situations.

"I urge parents not to compromise on this decision. The coach will have an enormous amount of exposure to a child at a crucial time in that child's life. I ask parents to measure the coach as they would a teacher, scout leader, or camp counselor, using the same standards for the desired treatment of their child. In my opinion, parents must be the watchdogs and react to things that bother them in the skating environment. I have observed that skating parents sometimes condone things happening to other children, or even their own, that they would never tolerate outside a rink. I feel we have a duty to protect our children, even though the intervention may not be politically correct.

"At a competition, I'm sometimes approached by frantic parents who are quite upset by their child's performance, judges' marks, or a coach's behavior. I ask that parent to first look at how the child is reacting. Is the child handling things OK? Usually skaters who don't skate their best or who don't like the placement get over it quickly, and are soon with their friends in the rink playing video games or running around the hotel. If your child is OK with a competition result, you should be, too. If a child is having a difficult time with the outcome, that's when the parents need to respond. Parents ideally remind their skaters that they love them unconditionally, whether they win or lose. Parents should help them to enjoy skating, even if things get difficult.

"I feel very sad for skaters when, in addition to the pressure of competing, they see their parents getting upset and even obnoxious at a competition, whether it's yelling at the child, the coach, the judges, or another skater. This is totally unacceptable to me. I try to point out at the parents' meetings, that no matter how good your skater gets, unless he or she becomes a National or Olympic Champion, no one will remember who that skater was within a couple of years after retirement from competition. However, the obnoxious parent will be remembered by others for behaving that way. Moreover, if total strangers recall your obnoxious behavior, I ask, what memories do you think your child will have of you some years from now?

"Other thoughts that I share with parents are to be realistic in their expectations. Be aware of the sacrifices required by skating and be prepared to pay the bills without attaching a condition like, 'Oh, we'll keep paying as long as you are winning.'

"Having your child away from your daily guidance is a big decision. If this is an option for you, it is a good time to step back and assess things. Hopefully, you are helping him or her, financially and emotionally, reach the highest potential in skating. Keep an attitiude that you are OK with things however they turn out, win or lose. The important thing is for your child to have a good experience and gain from it.

"The world of competitive skating can be challenging. It is truly an environment of excesses. Excesses in time, spending and pressure are the norm. Keeping things in perspective is very challenging. I remind parents that, in their efforts to be supportive of the child who is the skater, they should not forget the rest of the family. For us personally, although Jennifer's skating was very important, it was only one part of our family life.

"Our other daughter, Lisa, was deeply in love with a young man named Lance whom she had been dating since high school. Unfortunately, Lance was diagnosed with leukemia. I soon learned that the skating community can be like an extended family that truly comes together in a time of need. During Lisa's senior year of college (while Jennifer was a Junior Ladies national competitor), Lance's illness progressed to the point that, without a bone marrow transplant, he would certainly die. Palomares, Peninsula, Stockton, and St. Moritz skating clubs united and organized an incredible fund raiser called 'Chance of a Lifetime.' Without hesitation, the skating community came forward with donations, food, and volunteers, and put on a skating show for a standing room only crowd. The Ice Oasis in Redwood City donated the ice time, and every skater asked to participate did so, including Rudy Galindo and Kristi Yamaguchi.

"Over ten thousand dollars was raised. Sadly, a perfect match for Lance was never found. He lost his battle with cancer because of complications arising from a near-match transplant that took place ten weeks after he and Lisa were married. Despite this outcome, I know that the generosity of our skating community has given the gift of life to others in need of a transplant and our gratitude was more than we could express. My experience has been that the skating community has been a good and giving community.

"At this point in her life, Jennifer still enjoys skating. She recently skated in Kristi's Holiday on Ice Show in Salt Lake City. She looks forward to her third year in Sun Valley, skating as a member of the troupe for the ice shows. And, she is dating Jozef Sabovcik, a professional skater and the 1984 Olympic bronze medalist.

"Even with all the up's and down's of skating, Jennifer would still say it was worth it, and so would I."

Gail Erb, Skating Parent

"My daughter, Rebecca, started skating at the age of two and a half. She loved it and has pursued it ever since, reaching Nationals in pairs at age ten, and in singles at the age of thirteen. My older daughter, Cassie, also skated for some time and was involved in cheerleading, sports acrobatics, and ice hockey. My son, Matt, played football, soccer, baseball and ice hockey. Consequently, as a family, we have had a great deal of exposure to various competitive sports.

"I urge parents to encourage their children to try a variety of activities before settling on a single sport. This provides an opportunity to discover preferences and abilities as well as the level of commitment. Among the reasons children chose to participate in sports are to have fun, to acquire skills, to recreate, and to socialize. For some, gaining new skills is most important and for others, just the enjoyment of being part of the scene is most important. Hopefully, along the way, participation in sport builds coordination, confidence, and self-esteem.

"If your child is not extremely athletic and highly motivated, if your family is not very comfortable financially, and if your child likes many things, then I would advise you to avoid the higher levels of competitive skating. Skating is limiting. There may be little time or money left over to invest in other activities.

"If a child chooses to skate, parents need to be realistic about that child's abilities and goals. Make sure the goals are really attainable. There are many different levels of participation in this sport. Most children become interested in ice skating at a party or in the setting of group lessons. My eldest daughter didn't continue ice skating much beyond this point. Her goal was to obtain the highest level badge from the skating school, and she worked hard for it. When she earned that last badge to sew onto her jacket, we were very proud and she was very pleased with herself. This was a realistic goal for her in skating.

"As involvement progresses, many skaters enter showcase (artistic) competitions. These are fun events that feature props, jazzy costumes, contemporary music, and spotlights for the performers. Other skaters enter technical competitions, which are the ones that ultimately lead to Nationals and Worlds. Still others join a precision team or begin to learn ice dancing, search for a partner to make a pair, or switch to ice hockey. Whatever your child's abiltities, there is a place for him or her in skating.

"I offer a caution to those considering competitive skating at the higher levels. When just starting out, you have no idea where this is leading. It seems simple in the beginning. First one thing happens, then another. Then, one day, you find yourself rising from your warm bed at four in the morning. You leave the house in the dark with your breakfast in your lap, and you drive a considerable distance to a cold, dark rink for a freestyle session. Homework will be done in the car. Your child will dress for school in the car and that is where your dinner will often be eaten. It feels like training doesn't have a season, it just goes on and on. Skating is the most demanding sport we have experienced in terms of time, dedication, and money. Often ice is not readily available locally, and suitable ice for the high level competitor is not usually rented at normal times of the day. So you become abnormal, and skating consumes your child's life and the lives of your entire family. You must be sure that this is the decision that you want to make.

"If you and your child have made the commitment to pursue a skating dream, now you need to choose a coach. This is the most important decision you will make. Take your time deciding. You need to be certain that you and your child will be happy with your choice for a long time, because changes in coaching interrupt the continuity of your child's training and the security of your child. Visit the rink where you wish your child to train and observe the coaches in action with their students. Converse with other parents that you meet.

"Inquire about the coach's skating experience and method of teaching. Some coaches will prepare for and take your child to showcase competitions. Other professionals do not coach for artistic events. Some coaches are able to cut your child's music and choreograph the program while others may send you to another coach or outside person to assist with these matters. A few coaches work in an area of expertise, such as jumps and spins, and have no students of their own. Other coaches send students to them for special lessons. After your child has spent some years in skating, you may choose a famous coach with a proven name and record of accomplishment. Frequently, this will entail moving your child and perhaps part of your family to a different location. Famous coaches are often heavily committed to other high-level athletes and may not have time to spend with your child. Alternately, you may choose a coach in your area whose credentials are good but who has never produced a National, World, or Olympic champion. Yet, this coach knows the sport intimately and has all the resources necessary to guide your athlete. If this is what you choose, you may get a great deal of time and attention from your coach. A parent needs to ask questions about all these things and evaluate the circumstances.

"As you begin to work with the coach you have chosen, you need to develop an understanding about what things will be the responsibility of the coach and which will be yours as the parent. A parent may make suggestions from time to time, but not decisions. It is not up to the parent to decide what elements make up a program. The coach will make the final decision about the content, music, costume, and manner in which the skater will be presented. It is the coach's job, not the parent's job, to make corrections and criticisms. It is the parent's job to be on time, pay the bills in a punctual fashion, and provide the transportation, equipment, proper rest, and nutrition. Most importantly, the parent provides the love and support that will make it possible for the child to have the confidence to succeed.

"At the beginning of each season, the parents, athlete, and coach should have a meeting to plan the upcoming year. What are the new goals? What tests will be taken? What competitions will be entered? This is the opportunity to bring up any questions that you have. Do not hesitate to ask other questions as they arise. Issues are often complex and you cannot do your best to support your child's efforts if you do not have the facts. Issues that may be discussed are varied. Who will make the costumes? What new equipment needs to be purchased and what kind? What sort of off-ice training program will be followed? Is everything else working the way it should? Once the plan is in place, see it through. Changes in the middle of a season are particularly disruptive.

"Whether or not your child will attend summer camps, clinics, and seminars or seek extra help from other coaches or outside sources is the coach's decision. If a parent desires outside coaching for a skater, it is a common courtesy to communicate that to the coach.

"In experiencing skating with your child over the years, there will be exhilirating highs and devastating lows. One of the biggest problems facing the skating parent is how to help your child cope with these times. Self-esteem, mental health, and the development of your child as a total person (not just a skater) are the most important things to consider. What a parent needs to remember is to always give your child unconditional love and support. Let him know that you love and value him as a person, regardless of the outcome of the skating. When your child comes off the ice after a competition, make sure that your comments are positive, reflecting the good things you saw and the progress that was shown. Never cause your child to think that she embarrassed you, wasted your money, was less than adequate, or let you down in any way. Your child does not need any added pressure from you. In the higher levels of competitive skating, there is plenty of pressure without your adding to it.

"The level of skill and the intensity of the competition are much greater at Sectionals and Nationals. In order to prepare for this an athlete may choose to attend some competitions during the year that are judged by National and International judges and are attended by national-level competitors to learn what others around the country are doing at his or her level. Being a local star isn't the same thing as competing nationally. If you are approaching the sport with any expectations (like 'my child will win the Olympic Gold in four years'), then you are approaching skating with the wrong type of thinking and may be in for a huge series of disappointments. Don't put that kind of pressure on your child.

"Personally, I tend to be nervous when my child competes. I think the best thing to do if you feel this way is to stay away from her during the time immediately preceeding the competition. Discuss your feelings privately with your coach and let him know what time you will be dropping off your child for the event. As far as hair, makeup, and attire are concerned, prepare your child to be self-sufficient. Wish your child well and then disappear to fidget in private.

"There comes a time for every athlete when he hits the wall, and progress is not so easy as it was in the beginning. Remind the skater why she began to skate in the first place. Remind her to spend time enjoying her skating and practicing the things she does well. Talk about all the progress that has been made since the beginning and review the successes that she has had. Get out the old videotapes of your child's first competitions and point out the skills that have been acquired. Reminisce about all the places you've been together over the years of skating, all the friends you've made, and all the fun you've had. Remind your child to be thankful for her talent. Tell her how proud you are of her accomplishments.

"Encourage your athlete, who may be a young adult now, to participate in skating in other ways. Perhaps the child is old enough to assist with teaching Special Olympics classes or group lessons. Chances are that he has the skill to teach a beginner how to skate. Maybe he would like to learn to judge. Focus also on your child's other talents and abilitites. Make sure your child's life is full of other things to look forward to and begin to open up some doors for your child's life after skating. For most there is an end to skating competitively, and there needs to be attention given to planning for that time. During your child's skating years, therefore, take care not to limit your options or close any doors.

"If you have a child who has skated for a number of years and now wants to move on, it is nice to have a sense of completion. Encourage your child to take her remaining tests. The credentials will be useful later if she decides to coach, and the accomplishment may be impressive on a resume for college or a job.

"Along the way, if the sport of skating ceases to be fun for your child, you need to seriously question why, and make adjustments to the training or your thinking. Indications that the child may not be having fun include making excuses (illness, fatigue, vague aches and pains, too much homework) to skip skating sessions. You may have another clue if the child is coming off the ice upset day after day, if it is obvious that the spark and enthusiasm are gone, and if there is no will to practice, or if there is a fear of trying things. Fear of failure can be paralyzing.

"A child's frustration with acquiring a certain skill may be the reason. Perhaps the goals that were set no longer make sense to the child. The limitations that come with skating can make the child feel that she is missing other important things in life. She may feel that she has no life or her social life has suffered too much. The child may have coped with an injury for too long and feels that the pain will never go away. The injury is too difficult to overcome and there are other enjoyable things to do that take less time and are less painful.

"Or there may be a problem between the child and the coach. The child, however, may not be able to say directly, 'I don't know if I want to skate or compete any longer.' Now is the time to be honest. It is often hard for the parent, who has given up so much for the child to succeed, to accept the fact that skating is no longer what the child wants to do. On the other hand, the relationship between coach and skater may have ceased to work, and it may be time to move on. The skater may have outgrown the coaching style. The coach and skater may have become too close, so that the skater no longer treats the coach with respect. The skater's ego may have become bruised by the manner in which the coach has offered criticism.

"Nurturing a skater requires a great deal of patience on the part of the parent. Each skill will take a long time to master, sometimes years. At times you will see steady progress. At other times, your child will regress. Improvement is never steady. There will be hills and valleys. Physical growth and mental attitude, places of confidence, or places of self-doubt affect progress. Obviously, physical growth is a normal and desirable part of your child's journey through life. However, it can work against the child in terms of acquiring the skating skills. At times, your child will appear to get much worse before she gets better. This will not be the child's fault, but it may cause frustration, self-doubt, and worry. My daughter's first coach often said that skating is '90 percent mental,' and I have come to believe that. During the highs and lows, maintaining a positive attitude is the major ingredient of success.

"Growing up at the rink has been a positive experience for us. The years have not been wasted. Many of life's lessons have been learned. Among them are discipline, time utilization and good sportsmanship. Learning how to handle success and failure are important dividends of the sport. The athlete works with people of various ages, acquiring wisdom from those who are older and tolerance from those who are younger. The skater's friends may be of all ages.

"Being involved with my daughter and her skating, I can say that we have had wonderful times, made lifelong friends, and seen many places. Rebecca's skating has taken her to competitions all over the United States and to Europe. Traveling, meeting new people, observing other cultures, and seeing different parts of the country have given her a wonderful education that she will never forget."

Chapter Fifteen
Advice for Adult Skaters Who Just Want to Skate and for Those Who Want to Compete

Tracy: Adult skaters are involved in a wonderful sport at a point in their lives when most of those around them on the ice are younger. However, in the months and years to come, it is likely that there will be more adult skaters on the ice than ever before. In early 1998, USFSA had about 126,000 members, with 25 percent of these over the age of twenty-five. In addition to adults who skate, these USFSA members who are twenty-five and older include coaches, sport psychology members like Sam, USFSA officials, judges, and parents whose children skate. What is exciting is that the number of adults who skate is growing, and so are the venues for training, for performing in exhibitions, and for competing.

Adults who skate are interested in skating for the exercise and for the thrill of moving about in an athletic activity that combines both technical and artistic aspects. Although there are not specific numbers available, some percentage of adults skated as children and then left the sport for a variety of reasons before coming back. The remainder are adults who took up skating later in life.

Another distinction that can be made about adult skaters can also be found with skaters who are younger. Many adults skate recreationally and find this time quite satisfying. Other adults compete in a category relatively new to USFSA competitions—that of Adult, meaning twenty-five years of age or older.

The Adult National competition is so new that the first Adult National Championship took place in 1995. The fourth Adult National Championship was held in Oakland, California, in April 1998. The number of entries has increased markedly each year, and more than 600 adults entered in 1998.

Adults may have to look around a bit for a coach who will be responsive to their needs. In major metropolitan areas on the West and East Coasts or at large training centers, adults may find a coach for their singles lessons as well as coaching for ice dance and pairs.

In my limited experience of adult coaching, I find that these skaters are incredibly dedicated and want to achieve to the best of their ability. What I have observed about adult skaters so impresses me that I don't ever underestimate what an adult skater can do. As a coach, I find one of my initial tasks is to help adults set realistic goals, and then to make reasonable estimates of how long it will take them to learn specific skills.

Adults who received formal training as kids retain the muscle memories of skating and seem to be more comfortable bending their knees to get down into the ice. I find the biggest challenge for an adult learning to skate for the first time is bending the knees to attain proper form and control. Ballet training can be extremely helpful in developing the flexibility, balance, and coordination that skating demands, and for enhancing artistic grace.

For adults, I find that cognitive explanations really count when I am describing how to execute certain skills. I find myself incorporating all the sensory systems as I teach, and I have adults visualize, feel, and think about doing an element. I have observed that adults really tune in to their lessons, come on time, and use every minute. They are serious about their learning, whether they are skating recreationally or competitively. Because they have jobs, family responsibilities, and interests outside of skating, adults can find themselves distracted in ways that can be difficult for their skating. Decisions about whether to continue training can be agonizing because these people really love to skate! I recommend that adults think very carefully about how many hours per week they can devote to lessons, practice sessions, off-ice conditioning and the driving time necessary to get to these activities. A second issue is to evaluate carefully the financial resources needed to pursue skating when you are the one paying the bills.

In my opinion, adults skaters have the advantage of having lived inside their bodies longer and being able to better listen to the body's messages. I advise adult skaters to report something uncomfortable to me right away, or to see a physical therapist as soon as possible. If something hurts while skating or after leaving the ice, certainly a sharp pain, or twisting sensation, or burning, even cramping, pay attention to it. The knees and ankles seem to be especially vulnerable in adult skaters. Overuse injuries take on an even greater significance for the adult, I believe, because the recovery time can be long. I don't train adults differently than I do younger skaters, except in the *pacing* of training. I continually remind adults to allow plenty of time for acquiring skills, and to be patient as they learn elements for their programs if they compete.

I take off-ice conditioning seriously for my students. I strongly believe, however, that adults must be rigorous about off-ice training and must be certain that they warm up before skating in the morning. Allowing for extra time, ideally forty-five minutes to warm up and stretch, helps an adult prevent injuries. Cooling down is critical for adults, too.

Choreographer Chris Conte advises adults to concentrate more on the fundamentals. "It's important to train moves in the field. Adults, in my experience, may neglect these skills in being eager to compete, but don't let that happen. An edge class can be a nice outlet in moving around the ice to music, especially for those of you just starting to compete."

One of the reasons I can understand and be supportive of adults competing is because of my own personal experience in making a comeback as an adult. While competing as an elite pair skater, I got injured in a way that looked like it would end my skating for good. It was hard on me, and my brother Scott was devastated and angry. There was not enough time for me to fully recover in order for us to deliver the performance necessary at U.S. Nationals (that is, the Olympic Trials) to earn a berth on the 1980 U.S. Olympic Team.

I always had the support of my mother, whether as a thirteen year-old National title holder or as an adult skating in a show at a little theme park. My mother supported my decision to go back to skating when I was twenty-six. She encouraged me not to listen to nay-sayers who thought I was crazy to skate again in a serious way. She cheered me on as I competed in a World Professional competition in Spain, when I pursued professional skating in shows in Las Vegas, and when I was touring internationally.

What I respect so much in adult skaters now was what I had the chance to learn for myself. Adults decide for *themselves* why to skate, as I did at age twenty-six. I had a much different reason for skating at age sixteen. Adults like myself have to find the time and must set skating as their priority to make it happen. I see adults having that clarity and that deep sense of striving to be the best you are capable of in a very challenging sport. I know people who did not reach their personal best as amateurs when they were younger, but they later blossomed as adults and professionals. That is very exciting to me.

For adults who ask me about competing, I first suggest that they talk to adults who already compete in order to get an idea of what it's like. If the adult is convinced that competing is the right decision, I encourage him or her to set aside the time to be well-trained and to prepare programs carefully. I ask skaters to devote the hours necessary to polishing their routines, just as they would prepare for a major presentation or meeting at work. This preparation will do much to reduce their performance anxiety. So will the goal of skating their personal best during competition, even if they have declared a dream goal of placing or winning. An attitude of skating because you love it also helps adults keep their nerves under control.

And the adult competitions are so much fun! Whenever I've talked to a competitor, he or she comes back with wonderful stories about the good times with the other competitors and how supportive everyone was.

Right now, with so few adult competitions happening, a skater must be ready to travel and spend the money to go from one part of the country to another. That may not be possible for some. I also suggest that adult skaters ask around to see if they can skate at exhibitions where younger skaters are performing. You may create an opportunity for yourself to skate in front of an audience in this noncompetitive way.

What is it like for adults who compete? I asked my current students, Molly Johnson and Jay Kobayashi, and Molly's former partner, Steve Goldberg, to share their stories with you.

Molly Johnson
"I actually started skating on frozen ponds in New Hampshire after moving there when I was in eighth grade. In high school and college, I was a gymnast in a family that was involved in lots of sports. Later, my education took much of my time, but I craved some-

thing active. In my third year of medical school in Boston, I went skating at one of the many rinks around, met a coach, and got hooked on figure skating. It made me so happy to be doing something this challenging, and the mental, physical, and artistic combination really appealed to me.

"While an intern in Philadelphia, and during my medical residency at Stanford, I knew again I needed another outlet. I found the Ice Oasis in nearby Redwood City. At the time, Debi Thomas was skating there. I found a coach and started with one weekly lesson. By the time I began my dermatology residency, I had more time and flexibility in my schedule, so I went skating more often.

In 1988 my skating had to be stopped because of a difficult pregnancy. I stayed off the ice for five years enjoying my child. By the time she was four, I was missing the skating and started again, thinking I'd focus on ice dancing. It looked so easy to me and turned out to be so challenging! I passed my first six tests, but soon found myself wanting to try jumps.

I was fortunate to meet Jim Stewart, a coach who is extremely supportive of adult skaters. He was really into coaching older skaters and he took me seriously. He coached me in singles and also in pairs with my first partner, Steve Goldberg.

"Try to imagine our first pair competition, skating against teenage Juvenile pair teams at St. Moritz, a nonqualifying competition at the rink of the same name in Berkeley. I remember Darby Gaynor competing there with her partner. Because there were no age limits, Steve and I could show our moves along with these kids. For the most part, people were gracious to us.

"Competing with other adults was different when these competitions became available. Steve and I entered the second Adult National Championship in 1996, held in Lake Placid. Jim Stewart was preparing to move his family to Southern California, and I was upset about his leaving, but he promised to come with us to Nationals.

"Once there, I had so much fun. Adult skaters aren't so all-out competitive, because what each of us is doing out there is so hard. We cheered for each other and not once did anyone seem to try and psych out a competitor.

"Although Steve and I have had our share of nerves before, this time I was not nervous. I felt very relaxed. My singles skating had gone well (I won silver), and I was ready to show what we could do as a pair team. We had no goal in mind for how we might place. Fifteen pairs had entered and most competed. Steve and I went out to skate. Afterward, I felt it hadn't been our very best, but we were still happy with our performance.

"Steve told me later that he went to check out the results while I was off talking to a friend. He said he began by looking near the bottom of the list for our names and not being able to find them. He recalls that someone had to point out our names at the top of the list. We had come in first! Being Adult National Pair Champions was like a dream come true, but an idea I hadn't thought about before we skated.

"I will share this next part with you because I think it's instructive. With Jim Stewart gone, Tracy became our new coach, at Jim's suggestion. Steve and I trained hard to return to Adult Nationals as a pair team. Steve's wife was having their second child, his job got very pressured, and he reluctantly had to back out. I was very sad because pair skating was my first love. I went ahead and competed in singles, winning silver in the technical program.

"But it was the first time I had ever skated with expectations [what are called outcome goals in this book]. I won my preliminary round. I had people telling me I could win, that I should win. It is interesting for me to look back and realize that I was not relaxed as I skated that final round. I tripped in my footwork and had a terrible fall. I came in sixth overall but I was still happy with my skate. What I didn't realize until later was that I had let myself be affected by what others said, then put pressure on myself to win.

"And my skating life now? I skate singles with coach Julie Zusman-Lowndes. Tracy has coached me and my current partner, Jay Kobayashi, since May of 1997. Jay had skated Novice pairs when he was younger, but stopped skating for years. He returned to the sport and is getting his double jumps back after all those years. It's wonderful to skate pairs again with him.

"These days, I work as a dermatologist three and one half days a week at Kaiser Permanente Hospital. My daughters are now nine and two. I'll do anything not to miss a lesson, and I take the conditioning part of skating very seriously, spending plenty of time on my stretches. While I am quite flexible from being a gymnast and can still do the splits, I realize that some other adult skaters can't. I think we adult skaters can enjoy skating by using our strengths, whether artistic grace, creativity, or athleticism, and practice the other elements until we can put them out there.

"I do this because I love it, and I am so pleased that adult skating has taken off."

Jay Kobayashi

"It's very exciting for me to talk about my skating just after winning the Gold in Masters Pairs with Molly at the 1998 Adult National Championships. I also made it to the Championship Gold Men's event and ended up seventh. In my interpretive program, I received third place. I had put some pressure on myself, with the competition being local and also going into a pairs category with Molly. I am happy with how we did and pleased with my results.

"After studying dance for many years and dancing Polynesian shows in Hawaii and abroad for five years, skating seemed like the next thing to do. I was really inspired watching the 1984 Olympics with Brian Orser, Katarina Witt, and Torvill and Dean. I was actually twenty-three when I showed up at the rink for my first group lesson. I liked it and stayed with it, looking for people to work with. Now Julie Zusman-Lowndes is my singles coach and the person I've been with the longest. When it comes to planning my programs, I pick the music and come to her with a rough cut, my thoughts about costumes, and my concepts and ideas. We take it from there and plan the program.

"Back in the 1980s when I was beginning, there was no organized adult competitive circuit as there is now. Then there were few opportunities to try out a program in competition with other adults. After skating singles for two years, I wanted to try pairs and found a partner who was just ten years old to my twenty-five years! I looked much younger than twenty-five and we competed in Novice pairs at Regionals against *kids*. It was strange, but we qualified to go to Sectionals where we skated against some older teenagers, so it wasn't too weird.

"I wanted to find an older partner but hadn't. I stopped my training, moved to Hawaii, and got involved in Polynesian dance performance again in shows. Although I found a rink there, people were so laid back about skating that it was hard to take it seriously. I skated only occasionally. It wasn't until 1994 that I took up my training again, after moving back to California. The first adult national competition was being planned for 1995, and that interested me. I went to the 1996 and 1997 Adult Championships and did well. I like to be in the spot light and perform, so I was glad for the opportunity that the adult nationals gave me.

"Molly was the partner I'd been looking for to get into pairs again. It was challenging for us to skate together at first. She jumps and spins the opposite way, so we had to try things out and compromise a lot. Our work schedules didn't mesh, and the rink where Tracy trains us is an hour drive for me when the traffic isn't bad. I am a hair stylist and can finish with my clients as late as 10:00 P.M., so getting to the rink at 6:00 A.M. was really hard for me. Molly and I didn't have too many program run-through's done before we skated our event at the 1998 Adult Nationals. We still did pretty well because we are both so determined.

"People who skate as adults seem to do it for themselves, and that is the best kind of motivation. I see adults who started skating later than I did who have a motivation that is an inner drive. I see them improving.

"If an adult skater asked me for advice, I would say that you have to practice to make progress. Sure, ballet classes or other outside training may help, but it really is your determination to skate that makes it happen. I would say that adults should practice around other adults, and not ever give up.

"My future in competitive skating is uncertain right now. I know I want to teach adults who are beginners. And I am training for the 1998 Gay Games in Amsterdam, because this year figure skating is one of the events. I am really looking forward to it. I'd also like to work with a special needs child who wants to skate, just to see the enjoyment of skating happen for him or her."

Steve Goldberg

"I didn't begin figure skating until I was twenty-eight years old, just after I'd finished a master's degree at night while working full time. Although I thought pair skating was cool, I was unsure of the difference between ice dancing and pairs as I was learning the basics. Soon I ordered my first custom-made boots and got involved in private lessons, which I've pursued for seventeen years.

"My skating skills got a boost when I could skate three to four hours nearly every day for the year I taught in North Carolina while on a philanthropic grant program from Hewlett-Packard Corporation. I skated ISIA (a skating organization now called the Ice Skating Institute) there and started competing all over the region 'against the book' [as the only one in a category at a competition]. I skated singles, figures, and pairs with my first partner, a young teenager, Gloria Downey, who was also a first-time pairs skater. Her parents were very supportive, and we all became good friends.

"After returning to the San Francisco Bay Area, I met my next pair partner, adult skater Donna Fountain, who had been skating since the age of nineteen and who later passed her Junior freestyle test. We enjoyed practicing together so much that we soon began to train seriously. We did a lot of shadow skating and side-by-side jumps. We competed against much younger kids in ISIA events, and skated against the book at

ISIA Nationals in Dallas. There were not many adult pairs at that time, and we were quite well known.

"By this time, I had enrolled in an electrical engineering doctoral program at the University of California, Santa Barbara. I remained with my long-time employer, Hewlett-Packard, but still found time to skate and divided my training between Santa Barbara, Los Angeles, and San Jose. I even auditioned for Ice Capades. It seemed very appealing, but paid very little.

"I finished my degree and came back to Northern California full time, taking lessons from Tracy. I especially remember a pair clinic that was offered at the rink in Redwood City, where I got to skate with Ekaterina Gordeeva. My desire to do pairs was really strong, and I kept looking for the right partner. In 1993, I met Molly Johnson. She was very motivated and very athletic. After a short time discussing our mutual goals, we began training together three or four times per week.

"We worked very hard, first taking lessons from Jim Stewart, and then from Tracy. We even got lessons from Elena Bechke and Denis Petrov during the summer of 1996 at the San Jose Ice Centre. We had progressed to doing full overhead lifts, throw Axels, and death spirals. Molly and I competed whenever we could, often against the kids in the USFSA Juvenile pairs. At competitions, we cheered for them and they cheered for us.

"Looking back, my skating career has been one of the great highlights of my life. I never thought of myself as an athlete, because in school I hadn't done well with team sports. Skating has been the ultimate challenge requiring both physical prowess and artistic expression. After fifteen years, who would have thought that I would find myself with Molly, so well-matched and heading off to Lake Placid for the Adult National Championships. We never expected to win the pair title. It was a great experience.

"Skating for me is a wonderful outlet from work. I'm now the President and Chief Executive Officer (CEO) of Verticom, Inc., in Santa Rosa, California. My wife, Monica, totally supports my skating, and is good friends with Molly along with many of my other skating pals. We have two children, Aren, three, and Jennifer, one, who will certainly be spending lots of time at the ice rink keeping dad company. Right now, since my recent move, I am looking for a new partner and pursuing skating with the same enthusiasm I have felt for almost two decades. What a great sport for adults!"

Epilogue
Skate Your Personal Best— Putting It All Together

Sam: Throughout this book, Tracy and I have shared our philosophy of personal best skating with you, and our contributors have given you their thoughts and advice. As we bring this book to a close, I would like to answer three final questions that skaters and their parents often ask me.

Can I skate competitively and have a normal life?
My experience suggests this is possible under certain conditions that you and your family can create. If you have siblings, it means that your parents devote time to them and their interests, as well as to you and your skating. Another important condition that must be created to keep life normal is make certain that getting a good education remains a high priority for the skater so that career possibilities are not foreclosed.

Skating competitively and living normally means planning for life after skating, whether you wish to attend a university or trade school, obtain a job, or start coaching or trial judging. What also contributes to a normal life is spending time with friends outside of skating, whom you might meet at church or synagogue, through another sport besides skating, or through volunteer work or community service. Enjoying activities other than skating provides experiences to make life more meaningful.

Can I recover from a slump that has gone on for several months?
This is a challenging situation for any athlete, including skaters. Slumps can occur because of the long rehabilitation periods required to recover from serious injuries. In this case, talking with skaters who have come back after a devastating injury can be inspiring and help lift the recuperating skater out of the blues.

If the slump began after disappointing outcomes from the competition season, the skater may need to reevaluate his or her reasons for skating. If winning is the only thing that matters, then it can be very difficult to come back after feeling unhappy with the final results. The skater might benefit from shifting the value derived from skating for outcomes (like medals and money) to the process of skating and the good feelings that can come from learning more advanced elements. For skaters entrenched in the importance of winning, this may be impossible. The only other intervention that may help this skater shake off the slump is to switch to another kind of skating, such as moving from singles skating to pairs, or changing to ice dancing.

A skater who loves the feeling of skating and the thrill of learning something new has important values that aid in the recovery from a setback. These also happen to be the personal best reasons for skating that we discussed in our second chapter. It may not be too late for a discouraged skater to embrace these values.

What is a good course of action if I find that I am not physically capable of mastering certain elements like double or triple jumps?
I would suggest that you shift your emphasis to skating in a way that allows you to capitalize on those things you do well and enjoy. You may find it more comfortable to focus on developing artistic programs for competition. You might want to explore ice dancing or precision skating. *But please remember, there is a place for you in the sport.* It does not have to be high-level singles or pair competitive skating to be right or worthy of your time and efforts.

Adults skaters are wonderful role models for skating for the enjoyment of it. They also seem to enjoy their competitions a great deal. There seems to be so much less tension at the Adults Nationals than at U.S. Nationals. Adults are having fun while still skating their personal best and being competitive. They have enough life experience to know they can afford to cheer for one another. The big money in skating that puts so much pressure on athletes has not reached their level quite yet.

Skating presents many wonderful opportunities for all those who participate with a strong sense of committment to personal best. Enjoy the process and your own personal journey. Cultivate meaningful friendships. Allow yourself to learn from the mistakes you make—on and off the ice. Grow. Become completely committed to yourself and to going after the goals you have set, your dreams, and your desires. Celebrate your accomplishments in life and of course skating. Most of all, take the time to fully experience your personal best.

References

American Psychiatric Association. *Diagnostic and Statistical Manual of Mental Disorders*. Washington, D.C.: American Psychiatric Association, 1994.

Boitano, B. *Boitano's Edge, Inside the Real World of Figure Skating*. New York: Simon & Schuster, 1997.

Bower, S., and G. Bower. *Assert Yourself, A Practical Guide for Positive Change*. Boston: Addison-Wesley, 1975.

Brewer, B. W., and T. A. Petrie. "Psychopathology in Sport and Exercise." In *Exploring Sport and Exercise Psychology*, edited by J. L. Van Raalte and B. W. Brewer. Washington, D. C.: American Psychological Association, 1996.

Clark, N. *Nancy Clark's Sports Nutrition Guide Book*. 2d ed. Champaign, Ill.: Human Kinetics, 1997.

Danish, S. "Psychological Aspects in the Care and Treatment of Athletic Injuries." In *Sports Injuries: The Unthwarted Epidemic*, edited by P. E. Vinger and E. F. Hoerner. 2d ed. Littleton, Mass.: PSG, 1986.

Duda, J. L., A. E. Smart, and M. K. Tappe. "Predictors of Adherence in the Rehabilitation of Athletic Injuries. An Application of Personal Investment Theory." *Journal of Sport and Exercise Psychology*. 11(4) (1989): 367–81.

Fernandez, E., and D. C. Turk. "Overall and Relative Efficacy of Cognitive Strategies in Attenuating Pain." Paper presented at the 94th annual convention of the American Psychological Association, Washington, D. C., 1986.

Fisher, R., and W. Ury. *Getting to Yes*. New York: Penguin, 1981.

Flint, F. A. "The Psychological Effects of Modeling in Athletic Injury Rehabilitation." Ph.D. diss., University of Oregon, 1991.

Grove, J. R., R. M. L. Stewart, and S. Gordon. "Emotional Reactions of Athletes to Knee Rehabilitation." Paper presented at the annual meeting of the Australian Sports Medicine Federation, Alice Springs, April 1990.

Heil, J. *The Psychology of Sport Medicine*. Champaign, Ill.: Human Kinetics, 1993.

Martens, P. *The New York City Ballet Workout*. New York: William Morrow, 1997.

Melzack, R., and P. Wall. *The Challenge of Pain*. London: Penguin, 1988.

Orlick, T. *Psyching for Sport*. Champaign, Ill.: Leisure Press, 1986.

Pawlak, L. *The Appetite Brain-Body Connection*. Emeryville, Calif.: INR/Biomed, 1996.

Rotella, R. J. "Psychological Care of the Injured Athlete." In *The Injured Athlete*, edited by D. N. Kulund. Philadelphia: Lippincott, 1982.

Rotella, R. J., and S. R. Heyman. "Stress, Injury, and the Psychological Rehabilitation of Athletes." In *Applied Sport Psychology: Personal Growth to Peak Performance*, edited by J. M. Williams. Palo Alto: Mayfield, 1986.

Seligman, M. E. P. *The Optimistic Child*. Boston: Houghton Mifflin, 1995.

Taylor, J. "Intensity Regulation and Athletic Performance." In *Sport and Exercise Psychology*, edited by J. L. Van Raalte and B. W. Brewer. Washington, D. C.: American Psychological Association, 1996.

Unestahl, L.-E. *Better Sport by I. M. T.—Inner Mental Training*. Orebro, Sweden: Veje, 1982.

Wack, J. T., and D. C. Turk. "Latent Structures in Strategies for Coping with Pain." *Health Psychology* 3 (1984): 27–43.

Glossary

air position. The way in which a skater holds the body during the rotations of a jump.

artistic. A type of program in which choreography and interpretation of music are emphasized; one of the marks given in competition, and more correctly termed presentation mark.

Axel. An edge jump in which the skater takes off on the forward outside edge and lands on the opposite foot from the take-off foot. It is named for Norwegian skater Axel Paulsen, and is the only jump in which the skater takes off while skating forward.

Beillmann. A one-foot spin in which the skater reaches behind the head and clasps onto the blade of the free foot with both hands. It is named for Swiss skater Denise Beillmann.

camel. A spin in which the skater turns on a straight spinning leg while the free leg extends back, parallel to the ice. The upper body is parallel to the ice and the skater's whole body forms a T shape.

carriage. One of the factors judges evaluate when deciding the mark for presentation. It refers to the way in which a skater holds his or her body while moving about on the ice.

centered (centering). One aspect of the correct execution of a spin in which the skater spins in one place without drifting across the ice.

cheated jump. An example of incorrect jump technique in which the rotation begins before the takeoff, or too late and after the skater has landed.

check. In executing a spin or a jump, a maneuver intended to stop the skater's rotation. For example, a skater can check the arms by thrusting them out to the sides or check the free leg by extending it back.

choreography. The arrangement of elements, artistic movements, and connecting steps set to a musical selection for a skater's program.

clean. To skate a program or element without mistakes.

combination jump. Usually two jumps in which the skater takes off from the same edge in the second jump that was used for landing in the first. Combination jumps are named for the number of rotations in each jump, for example, a double-double. Triple-triple jumps are becoming more common.

combination lift. In pair skating, an element in which a change occurs in the lady's air position or the way she is held by the man.

combination spin. A spin involving a change in position, and/or a change of the spinning foot.

connecting step. Footwork that links together the elements in a program.

costume. The outfit worn by a skater during a competition program.

crossover. A move in which the skater skates in a curved direction, either forward or backward, by repeatedly crossing one foot on the inside edge of the blade over the opposite edge of the other foot.

cut. To record and edit the music used in a program.

death spiral. In pair skating, an element in which the man executes a pivot on the toe pick while holding the lady with one hand and turning her around him in a spiral. The lady lowers her head toward the ice without touching it and must not allow her free hand to make contact with the ice.

deduction. In the judging of a program, a judge subtracts some portion of the top mark for a skater's error in executing an element, or for omiting a required element, or for a violation of the rules, such as using a prop incorrectly in an artistic program.

discipline. One of the specialty types of training within the sport of figure skating. At the U.S. National Championships, the disciplines represented are figures, ladies' singles, men's singles, ice dancing, and pair skating.

dismount. In pair skating, the descent from a lift, during which the lady comes back down on the ice.

double (double jump). A jump in which the skater makes two revolutions, or two and one-half in the Axel.

edge. The part of the blade that has contact with the ice. This can be the outside or inside edge.

edge jumps. Of the six jumps, the three (loop, Salchow and Axel) in which the skater takes off from the edge of the take-off foot without the assistance of a toe pick by the other foot.

element. A technical component in a program; a major skill learned by skaters in singles and pairs skating, for example, a jump.

elite (elite level). A level in sport designating that the athlete has reached an international, world, or Olympic status through national ranking and age eligibility.

figures (school figures; compulsory figures). One discipline in figure skating in which the skater skates a pattern on the ice that is judged for accuracy. No longer a mandatory part of championship skating in major competitions, skaters train in figures as a discipline in its own right.

flip. A jump in which the skater begins from a three turn and uses the assistance of the toe pick on takeoff.

flood (also called ice make). The time during which the ice in a rink is shaved clean and resurfaced with water that quickly freezes to form a smooth surface.

flying spin. A spin that a skater begins with a leap into the air before spinning.

footwork. The steps in a program, which may be inspired by dance movements, that give a skater the chance to demonstrate skill, quickness, grace, and creativity.

free foot. The foot that is not touching the ice.

free leg. The leg that is up and away from the ice.

free skate. Another name for the long program, in which skaters can freely choose the choreography that showcases their skills. The free skate is four minutes long for ladies' singles, and for pairs and men this program is four and one half minutes in length at the championship level.

freestyle. The skating in mens' and ladies' singles that involves elements and footwork with a musical accompaniment. Short and long programs, as well as exhibitions and show programs, are all considered freestyle skating, as opposed to figures. Also, the session in which skaters practice their elements and moves.

gold medal. The highest test that a skater can pass at a certain level in each of the skating disciplines.

ice dancing (ice dance; dance). A discipline in figure skating that features a male and female team performing dance maneuvers. Dance is distinguishable from pair skating in that Ice Dancers do not execute overhead lifts or jumps.

inside edge. The side of the blade corresponding to the inside of the foot.

International Skating Union (ISU). The organization that oversees international competitions such as the World Championships and skating events at the Olympic Games. The ISU sets rules for participation and for the judging of competitions. ISU member nations have their own national organizations (like the United States Figure Skating Association) that oversee competitions and prepare national teams for ISU events.

judge. A trained person responsible for assigning marks for a skater's performance in a competition.

jump. An element that involves the skater springing up into the air with both feet off the ice and turning at least one-half turn or revolution. The six jumps are distinguished by the take-off edge and landing foot. A skater lands on the back outside edge in all six types of jumps. Three of the jumps—the Lutz, toe loop and flip—are toe pick-assisted jumps in which the skater pushes into the ice with the toe pick of the free leg for added momentum.

jump sequence. A series of jumps, usually more than two, in which the skater executes steps, half-revolution jumps, or turns in between the elements. A jump sequence is not a jump combination.

Kilian position. In ice dancing and pair skating, a position in which the partners skate side by side in the same direction.

kiss and cry. The area outside the rink where a skater and coach sit and wait for the results to be posted.

landing. The touchdown of a jump.

landing edge. During the landing of a jump, the edge of the blade on which the skater touches down.

layback spin. During this spin, the skater arches the back and stretches the head back as far as possible.

level. The division based on test level in which a skater competes, such as Novice or Senior.

lift. In pair skating, an element in which the man elevates the lady up off the ice.

lobe. An arc skated on the ice forming at least one-third of a circle.

long program (artistic program). The free skate program in competition, with some required elements and the freedom to choreograph in such a way that the skater's skills and artistic flair are obvious to the judges. For ladies, this program is four minutes long at the championship level, and for men and pairs, this program is four and one-half minutes long.

loop. An edge jump in which the skater takes off on the back outside edge and lands on the same foot used for takeoff.

Lutz. A toe-pick assisted jump in which the skater takes off on the back outside edge and lands on the same foot as the toe-assisted takeoff. It is often distinguishable from the other five types of jumps because it is a counter-rotation jump, with the skater curving to the right on the takeoff but rotating left. It is named for Austrian skater Alois Lutz.

mark. A judge's evaluation of a skater's performance during competition, either for technical or artistic merit.

mental training (mental skills). A set of skills, such as focusing or being able to relax or energize at will, that assist an athlete in learning physical skills and in competing well.

Mohawk. A turn done on two feet in which the skater changes feet when changing direction.

moves in the field (moves). A part of the USFSA test structure. Skills that aid a skater in developing a command of interconnecting steps and turns at all levels.

optimism. A way of explaining events, good and bad, that helps keep a person hopeful, persistent, and looking for ways to solve problems.

outcome goal. A goal that focuses on results or outcomes, such as winning medals or making money from skating. A skater has less than total control over outcome goals.

outside edge. The side of the blade corresponding to the outside of the foot.

pair spin. In pair skating, an element in which the partners are skating on identical lobes, meet in the center, and grab hold of one another while each is spinning on one foot.

patch. The session in which skaters practice figures.

performance goal. A goal that focuses on what a skater has more control over, such as how well to skate in a competition or the attitude that the skater maintains during a practice session or competition.

pessimism. A way of explaining events, good and bad, that discourages a person and brings on hopelessness, an urge to give up, and sometimes depressed mood.

pivot. A move in which the skater plants the toe pick of one skate in the ice and circles around it on the other skate.

pop. Skating slang for decreasing the number of rotations that were planned for a jump by checking the rotation sooner. "Popping a triple" means that the skater actually executed a double or single jump of the same type.

practice ice. As part of the schedule for a competition, the time reserved for a particular group of skaters to practice their programs.

precision skating (precision team). A discipline in figure skating that involves groups of skaters executing routines in formations.

presentation mark (mark for artistic merit). The evaluation given by a judge for a skater's artistic performance during a competition. The ISU and USFSA rules declare that the judge must consider the following seven factors when awarding the artistic mark: harmonious composition of the program as a whole and its conformity with the music chosen; variation of speed; utilization of the ice surface; easy movement and sureness in time to the music; carriage and style; originality; and expression of the character of the music. There is one additional factor evaluated in pair skating, that of unison of the skating.

program. A package of elements, footwork, artistic aspects, costume, and style that are integrated into a piece of music selected for a competition or an exhibition.

quad (quadruple jump). A jump with four revolutions or, in a quadruple Axel, four and one-half revolutions. Quadruple jumps are becoming more common in elite competitions.

quality edges. A term referring to skating in a way that no rasping or scraping sounds are heard, indicative of sharp, clean edge movements on the ice.

referee. The official who oversees the work of the judges at a competition.

regional. For competitive figure skating, the United States is divided into three sections, each of which is further divided into three regions. The three regions in the Eastern Section are the New England Region, the South Atlantic Region, and the North Atlantic Region. The three regions of the Midwestern Section are the Upper Great Lakes Region, the Eastern Great Lakes Region, and the Southwestern Region. The three regions of the Pacific Coast Section are the Southwest Pacific Region, the Northwest Pacific Region, and the Central Pacific Region. The regional competition is the first in a series of two qualifying competitions leading to the U.S. Nationals for Novice, Junior and Senior levels.

required element. An element that must be included in the short program at a particular level in each discipline of figure skating. The ISU sets these requirements each year.

rocker. A turn done on one foot in which the skater maintains the same edge.

run-through. To practice a program.

Russian split. A jump in which the skater thrusts the legs up and out to form a very wide V split position while leaping into the air. The arms are stretched out toward the toes and the skater looks straight ahead.

Salchow. An edge jump in which the skater takes off on the back inside edge and lands on the opposite foot from the take-off foot. It is named for Swedish skater Ulrich Salchow.

sectional. For competitive figure skating, the United States is divided into three sections, the Eastern Section, the Midwestern Section and the Pacific Coast Section. The sectional competition is the second in a series of two qualifying competitions leading to the U.S. Nationals for Novice, Junior, and Senior levels.

short program (technical program). The two minute and forty second program at the Junior and Senior level that includes required elements and is skated by ladies, men, and pairs.

showcase. A noncompetition program skated for the enjoyment of an audience.

side-by-side jump. In pair skating, an element in which both partners execute a jump simultaneously in a matched pattern.

single (single jump). A jump in which the skater makes one revolution, or one and one-half in the Axel.

sit spin. A spin in which the skater drops down into a sitting position and spins on one foot while the free leg is fully extended.

skating foot. The foot in contact with the ice.

skating leg. The leg that bears the skater's weight.

solo spin. In pair skating, when the partners execute the same spin side by side in unison.

spinning foot or spinning leg. In a spin, the leg and foot on which the skater is turning.

spiral. A move in which the skater's free leg is extended up and behind.

spiral sequence. A set of spirals executed in patterns across the ice.

split. A position of the legs in a jump or lift in which the legs are stretched far apart, either out to the side or with one leg extending to the front and the other to the back.

step sequence. A series of steps and turns performed across the ice surface in time to the music in a program.

stroking. A way of moving across the ice by pushing off on the inside edge of one foot and then the inside edge of the other foot, alternating feet to reach good speed.

style. One of the factors judges evaluate when deciding the mark for presentation. It refers to the gracefulness and flair with which a skater moves.

take-off edge. In a jump, the edge from which the skater propels himself or herself into the air.

technical mark (mark for technical merit). The evaluation given by a judge for a skater's technical performance during a competition. The ISU and USFSA rules declare that the judge must consider the following four factors when making the technical mark: difficulty of the performance; variety; cleanness and sureness; and speed.

technical program. The short program that includes required elements.

test judge. A judge who evaluates skills at a certain level in a discipline in figure skating. A judge who judges in a competition first spends time as a test judge.

three turn. A turn done on one foot in which the skater rotates the upper body, then checks the rotation to reverse direction. The imprint left on the ice from this maneuver looks like the number three and gives this turn its name.

throw jump. In pair skating, an element in which the man gives the lady momentum on her jump by propelling her away from him.

toe loop (toe). A toe-pick assisted jump in which the skater takes off from the back outside edge and lands on the same edge that was used for the takeoff.

toe pick. The front end of the blade on a figure skate that looks like a serrated knife.

toe-pick assisted jumps. Of the six jumps, the three (toe loop, flip, and Lutz) in which the skater takes off from the edge of the take-off foot with the assistance of a toe pick maneuver by the other foot.

trial judge. A judge who sits in with judges who are judging skaters' performances in a competition. The trial judge's marks are not counted but are reviewed for accuracy and fairness.

triple (triple jump). A jump in which the skater makes three revolutions, or three and one-half in the Axel.

twist. In pair skating, a move executed during the dismount in which the lady turns rapidly during her descent to the ice.

two-footed landing. In a jump, the skater incorrectly lands on two feet or lands on one foot but puts the other foot down to maintain balance and avoid a fall.

unison. In ice dancing or pair skating, when the partners skate the same elements or moves at the same time, either in shadow skating or in mirror image skating form.

upright spin. A spin in which the skater is spinning on a straight leg with the free leg crossed in front of the spinning leg.

warmup. The minutes before competitors take their turns performing their programs. In the warmup, several competitors are on the ice together preparing to skate for the judges.

Worlds. The annual international competition also known as the World Championships.

Zamboni. The U.S. slang for the machine that resurfaces the rink ice by scraping it and applying more water, which rapidly freezes into a newly smooth surface. There are other manufacturers of this equipment.

Index

Index of Authors Cited

About the Authors

Sandra Foster, Ph.D., is a performance enhancement psychologist based in San Francisco. Her work focuses on teaching high performance skills to people in sport, business, and the performing arts. She is an executive coach and has worked with the decision-makers of several of Silicon Valley's leading companies. She is a sport psychology consultant certified by the Association for Advancement of Applied Sport Psychology (AAASP) and member of the U.S. Olympic Committee Sport Psychology Registry. She is a consulting associate professor at Standard University. She specializes in working with skaters, golfers, practitioners of martial arts, and dancers, and has been published in *Skater's Edge*, *American Fencing*, and *At Work: Stories of Tomorrow's Workplace.*

Tracy Prussack is a figure skating coach with thirteen years' experience. She instructs students from beginner to advanced levels. Her students have competed and won medals at national and international competitions. Her skating career includes being a USFSA gold medalist and international medalist. She is a former U.S. National Junior Pair Champion. Her nine-year fight back from a pre-Olympic injury resulted in a comeback at the 1989 World Professional Championship. She was the 1998 U.S. Open Professional Challenge Cup Champion in both singles and pairs. She and her colleague Louis Vachon were nominated by the Professional Skaters Association (PSA) for the 1997 Future Generation Coach award.

Also in the Personal Best Series:

Skate Your Personal Best—The Skater's Companion

a planner and journal
for your annual competition season or recreational skating year

$26.95 enclosed wirebound 0-945213-28-X
128 pages, erasable board with rink diagram, 7"x 10"

Used to implement the techniques and philosophies described in
Skate Your Personal Best. Everything from exercises for managing distractions
and fears to planning programs and schedules. Saved each year
it is transformed from a planner into a skating diary.

Skate Your Personal Best—Sound Advice

Audio tapes for controlling nervousness,
mentally preparing for competitions, and getting to sleep

$19.95 audio 0-945213-29-8
Two 60 minute tapes

Companion audio tapes to help with motivation, inspiration, and relaxation.